Stephen Chalke was born in Salisbury in 1948. He has worked for many years in adult and higher education and is a keen cricketer with The Journeymen, a wandering side, and South Wraxall, a small village in West Wiltshire. He has written two previous books on cricket: *Runs in the Memory* (1997), which was chosen by Frank Keating as his Book of the Year in The Guardian and by E.W. Swanton as one of his six favourite cricket books, and its sequel *Caught in the Memory* (1999). Both recapture county cricket's past through the memories of its participants, a technique which he has developed here in this book.

Bryan 'Bomber' Wells was born in Gloucester in 1930. An off-spin bowler, he played cricket for Gloucestershire from 1951 to 1959 and for Nottinghamshire from 1960 to 1965. A printer by trade, he now lives in retirement in Gloucester. He has developed a reputation for his amusing story-telling at Cricket Societies up and down the country, but he also has strong views on cricket past and present, and this mix of humour and telling comments is captured here in this book. His previous memoir *Well, Well, Wells* (1981) was published in a limited edition of 500 and is now a much sought-after volume in the second-hand book market.

Ken Taylor was born in Huddersfield in 1935. A batsman, occasional bowler and brilliant fielder, he played cricket for Yorkshire from 1953 to 1968 and in three Test matches for England. He played football as a centre-half in the old First Division for Huddersfield Town, once scoring four goals against West Ham United. He trained as an artist at the Slade and works in Norfolk as a teacher of art. He collaborated with Stephen Chalke on both *Runs in the Memory* and *Caught in the Memory* and is building up a collection of portraits of sportsmen.

Susanna Kendall was born in High Wycombe and now lives in Bath. She trained as an artist at Camberwell School of Art and has illustrated a number of children's and natural history books. She is the artist attached to the Ways With Words Literary Festivals, where she sketches speakers, and she also specialises in detailed botanical portraits and landscapes.

ONE MORE RUN

Gloucestershire versus Yorkshire

Cheltenham, August 1957

Stephen Chalke

talking with

Bryan 'Bomber' Wells
(of Gloucestershire)

illustrations by Ken Taylor
(of Yorkshire and England)
and Susanna Kendall

FAIRFIELD BOOKS

Fairfield Books
17 George's Road, Fairfield Park, Bath BA1 6EY
01225-335813

First published 2000

ISBN 0 9531196 2 9

Printed and bound in Great Britain by
Redwood Books, Trowbridge

For

Mary Wells

CONTENTS

ILLUSTRATIONS

There are six portraits of cricketers by **Ken Taylor**:

Tom Graveney	21
Sam Cook	49
Johnny Wardle	65
Jimmy Binks	82
Fred Trueman	95
Arthur Milton	105

Colour prints of these and many other portraits are available from Ken Taylor at The Red House, Stody, Melton Constable, Norfolk NR24 2EB.

These portraits are interpretations of black-and-white photographs. The ones of Tom Graveney, Fred Trueman and Johnny Wardle are by **Ken Kelly**, and Ken Taylor and the publishers would like to thank him for granting permission for the photographs to be used in this way. Ken Kelly was for many years the world's leading cricket photographer, and a collection of his work has been published under the title **Cricket Reflections** (David & Charles, 1985). He is the curator of the museum at Edgbaston.

The original photograph of Sam Cook belongs to Carol Cooper and has been interpreted with her permission. The ones of Jimmy Binks and Arthur Milton appeared in the now defunct Playfair Cricket Monthly magazine. The publishers have tried to find out the copyright owner of these photographs, and if any photographic source believes that they are theirs they should contact the publishers.

Other photographs reproduced in the book are with the kind permission of Gill Ford, David Watkins, Gloucestershire County Cricket Club and the Gloucestershire Echo.

The scorecard and the page of the scorebook are reproduced with the kind permission of Gloucestershire County Cricket Club.

The other illustrations, including the one of 'Bomber' Wells on page 9, are by **Susanna Kendall**.

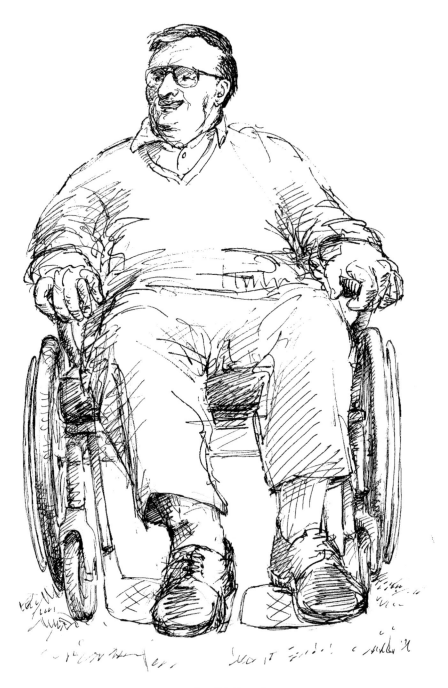

Bomber Wells today

CRICKET AT CHELTENHAM

Starting in 1999

"Would you like a cup of tea?"

An elderly man sits in a wheelchair to one side of the scorebox, his eyes twinkling through thick glasses.

"No, it's all right, thank you, Bomber."

"Mary, pour Stephen a cup of tea."

It is July 1999. The last summer of the century, the last summer of the old-style County Championship, and today's teams, Gloucestershire and Worcestershire, are both struggling for places in next summer's Division One.

"Have you been to Cheltenham before? It's a lovely place to watch cricket, isn't it? Ab-so-lute-ly su-perb."

The Gloucester vowels stretch out every word, and his face is lit up with the prospect of a good natter. But his eyes never leave the cricket.

"Did you read that article in the Telegraph?"

He passes Monday's edition, with its piece on Festival Cricket by Michael Henderson. *'Cheltenham and Scarborough are probably the best two places in England, outside Lord's, to watch cricket. ... Just going there makes one feel well-disposed towards the world.'*

I have driven up the A46, a winding road lined by farm fields, through the little towns of Nailsworth and Stroud, then over Painswick Hill and down all the way to the grand and prosperous town of Cheltenham, nestled among these Cotswold Hills.

I park in a large field and walk along the road, entering at a gate at the side of Cheltenham College's Victorian Gothic gymnasium, with its twin steeples and its yellow brickwork broken by red-and-black patterning. Between the steeples a balcony runs, with a white wooden trellis, behind which the press sit and watch the game side-on. For most of the remaining three sides of the ground there are marquees, broken by occasional tiers of open seating. Beyond them on the far side stands a hospital, with great Ionic columns, and to the left the College's Chapel and Hall, a vista of Victorian architecture disturbed only by the Eagle Star office block that rises high behind them.

A gentle breeze accompanies the morning sunshine as, all round the ground, chairs are unfolded and picnic baskets placed carefully on the grass. In marquees wine glasses are polished, beer kegs are set up, and caterers deliver trays of food. A caravan, with a display of second-hand books, sports a window smashed yesterday while the players practised, and a local car dealer stands beside a row of the latest models. There are people everywhere. A good crowd in an age when county cricket struggles for an audience.

I look down at my programme. Price, 50p. The Abbey Business Equipment Cheltenham Cricket Festival. The PPP Healthcare County Championship. The match ball sponsored by Hazelwoods Accountants.

"Back when I played in the fifties," Bomber tells, "there was one big marquee for entertainment by the Cheltenham Council, perhaps a smaller one for the Constitutional Club. And the rest was open seating."

An aerial view of the ground in the 1950s

Gloucestershire have asked Worcestershire to bat, but there is nothing in the pitch for the bowlers. The openers accumulate steady, unspectacular runs. On the balcony of the gymnasium Michael Henderson pens his first paragraph. *'Hafeez spread out his 32 runs carefully, like a miser counting his coins, and a good few eyelids had dropped by the time he edged a catch to Russell.'* It is the sort of morning when your mind wanders and the shadows of the past start to drift across the scene.

"My friend Percy is 93," Bomber says, "and he can remember when the local farmers turned up with their hay wagons and placed them all round the boundary for the people to sit on. There was a big rabbit show for the children, and in the intervals there was this man who'd come out with his performing dog. People would be walking round the ground selling glasses of cider and bread and cheese, and you could hear everybody drinking away in the beer tent. It was a huge social occasion."

"So where did Percy come from?"

"He's lived in Upper Slaughter all his life. He'll tell you how, when he was a boy, he was in the choir there. This vicar, the Reverend Hadrow - he was cricket mad - he brought them all over. They walked to Bourton, took the train to Leckhampton, then they walked all the way to the ground."

John Light, Chairman of the Gloucestershire Exiles, appears at Bomber's side.

"Pull up a pew, my friend. Would you like a cup of tea?"

Born in 1940, the son of a Cotswold forester, John can recall the pull of the Festival when he was growing up. "We were living at Rodmarton, near Tetbury. I would cycle into Cirencester, leave my bike by the Swan pub, and catch the double-decker bus that came from Swindon. It went up the road through North Cerney, and there were North Cerney people on the bus who'd got on before Cirencester. They'd come down earlier in the morning, paid the extra fare, so as not to risk waiting at North Cerney for the bus to go straight through full.

"I came here first in 1949. The first ball I saw, Jack Crapp was out. I thought he was bowled. For forty years I thought that. Then one day I said to Dad, 'Do you remember that first ball I saw at Cheltenham, when Crapp was bowled by Laker?' 'No, he wasn't,' said Dad. 'He was stumped.' I looked it up, and he was right. It happened so quickly."

His father Charles's memory runs back many more years. "The first time I saw cricket here was in 1926, when I was thirteen. The Australians came. Gregory, a very tall fast bowler, I'd never seen anybody like that before. Then in '29 I came to see Hampshire, but that was on the town ground."

"And how did you get here?"

"We cycled. From Sheepscombe. There was a big yard where you could park your bike all day for twopence. Dennett, the old Gloucestershire spin bowler, was on the gate, collecting the money."

George Dennett. At that time he would have been one of the ten greatest wicket-takers in the history of cricket, and he was collecting coins at the gate.

"Did you have to lock your bike?"

"God, no. You didn't even lock it when you went to the pictures at Cirencester."

"What sort of people came?"

"All the people from the villages. In those days it always started on the second Saturday in August. You went through harvest fields to get to Cheltenham, and that seemed right. Not like now, when they're playing in the middle of July. And there were always a lot of country vicars, but then there were so many of them in those days. Now our vicar does four or five villages."

"So were you here in 1928 when Hammond had that wonderful week?"

Wednesday to Friday against Surrey, Hammond scored 139 and 143, took Jack Hobbs' wicket and held a world record ten catches in the match. Then on the

Saturday morning against Worcestershire, he took nine for 23 and caught the tenth off Charlie Parker. *'He did not bowl fast, but he appeared to 'bump' the ball a good deal,'* is the summary in the Gloucestershire Echo, and the only words the reporter can get out of him are, 'The wicket was a bit tricky.' Not too tricky, though, to prevent him appearing in the afternoon and making a watchful 80. On Monday he added another six wickets.

"He had such grace," Charles recalls, "and I've never seen a better bowling action. Of course a lot of the local chaps knew him from his time at Cirencester Grammar School. I never saw Bradman, but Hammond was certainly the best cricketer I ever saw."

Bomber beams. "I was talking to an old chap the other week, and he'd seen Bradman. 'He was just an accumulator of runs,' he said. 'But when you saw Hammond you saw the most majestic creature who was ever put on this earth.'"

"But were you there, Charles, on the Saturday, when he got the nine wickets and the 80?"

"We only had the one day off work each week, you see. If we came here we had to miss our own match, and we were playing at Ampney Crucis. But I remember getting back to North Cerney on the bus, and we met our secretary. He was an older man, he always came here to the festival, and we asked him all about it. 'Oh,' he said, 'it was rather dull.' Those were his very words. He reckoned Hammond's 80 was slower than usual."

"Tom Graveney first saw first-class cricket here," I say. I have been to see Tom at his golf club, high on a hill beyond Leckhampton. Tom Graveney, who was Gloucestershire's greatest post-war batsman.

"I saw the West Indies at Cheltenham in 1939," he told me. "I was twelve, just started at Bristol Grammar School, and my brother Ken and I got the train up. We took our sandwiches and sat on the grass. Charlie Barnett bowled this bouncer, and George Headley hit it harder than I've ever seen a ball hit. He absolutely smashed it. And he just tipped a bail off. Hit wicket, bowled Barnett, five."

'Festival cricket,' Michael Henderson writes. *'It's where the heart of county cricket beats most strongly. ... where people renew friendships left off the previous summer ... quaff pints in tents ... and rediscover why they fell in love with cricket.'*

"The village cricketers all used to come here," Charles Light recalls. "Some years the local fixtures had to be cancelled. And the beer tent did good business. Flowers Bitter was seven pence. Six pence was the price of beer for years. But Flowers was better than Stroud or Ciren Beer. It was worth the extra penny."

"I remember the West Indians in 1950," his son John says. "There was a tremendous queue to get in. It was like Swindon playing Arsenal in the Football League Cup Final in 1969. And I do remember Ramadhin."

Gloucestershire, all out for 69 and 97. Ramadhin, eight for 15 and five for 36. Poor little Andy Wilson, the wicket-keeper. His team mate Sam Cook made sure his batting that match was never forgotten. "Cooky told that lovely story," Bomber says. "In the dressing room they were saying they couldn't read Ramadhin, and

Andy Wilson said, 'Piece of cake,' something like that. First innings the ball pitched outside the off-stump, Andy padded up, and it turned and bowled him middle stump. Second, it pitched outside the leg, he never played a shot, and it hit his off-stump out of the ground. And they laughed. He never lived it down. He could read him, and he got a king pair."

"I was the only one who got double figures in both innings," Tom Graveney recalls with pride. 19 and 23, to be precise.

"I think Graveney was down the other end, facing Valentine most of the time," John suggests. "The first ball he faced from Ramadhin, he was bowled. That's my memory of it."

"In the first innings possibly," Tom says. "I remember sweeping Alf Valentine for a couple of fours to get to 15 or 20. But I played Ram in the second. I remember seeing the ball spinning through the air."

"It bucketed down in the morning," Bomber recalls. "Then the sun came out, and Ram went through us. I was there with my brother Dave. Morty played, didn't he?"

John Mortimore, the 17-year-old off-spinner, making the first appearance of a Gloucestershire career that will stretch a quarter of a century to 1975. *Mortimore showed considerable promise,'* Wisden records, but Bomber and his brother Dave are less impressed. "Walcott hit him so far and so often, it was embarrassing. He actually hit him into the hospital grounds. I remember thinking, 'If I were bowling, he wouldn't do that to me.'"

"So did you think you were good enough to play for Gloucestershire?"

"Oh, no. The Gloucestershire team were on a pedestal to me. I never dreamt I'd play county cricket."

Yet within the twelve month he was out on the square - "the hallowed turf," as he calls it - taking Glamorgan wickets in tandem with Sam Cook. 1951, the summer of his debut.

It was in 1951 that George Emmett hit 146 here against Worcestershire. "One of the best innings I've ever seen," Tom Graveney says. "It was turning square, Roly Jenkins and Dick Howorth were bowling, and he kept sweeping the ball. George swept on length, you see, not direction."

"He was good to watch," Charles Light says. "A small man, all wrist."

"He hit Roly Jenkins for three successive fours," Bomber tells, "and, when the clapping died down, Roly walked down the pitch, put his hands on his hips. I can see it now. I was twelfth man, and I was sat with most of the cast of the Archers; they were all cricket mad. Roly looked at him and said, 'Emmett, if you don't like me, that's fair enough. But for God's sake, don't keep taking it out on the ball.' You should have heard the laughter all round the ground."

Roly Jenkins. There is a smile on every face at the mention of his name.

"I've got a tape," I say, "of a radio interview he recorded just before he died."

"When they went to bed together, my mum and dad," Roly starts, "my dad used to say, 'Shall we go to sleep or what?' And she said, 'What?', and that's why I'm here."

Roly is a great one for learning up poems and sayings, and in this interview he recites Lord Harris's 1931 letter to The Times: *'Cricket. It is freer from anything sordid, anything dishonest, than any other game in the world. To play it keenly, generously, honestly, is a moral lesson in itself, and the classroom is God's air and sunshine. Foster it, my brothers, protect it from anything that will sully it, so that it will be in favour with all men.'* Roly draws breath. "I wonder what he'd do in his grave if he could see what's going on in the game today."

"Mary and I were watching a game at the King's School the other evening," Bomber tells. "The Sixth Form against the Masters. People were clapping one another. 'Splendid catch, Mr Robins,' the Headmaster said. Then somebody dropped one: 'Gallant effort.' They were words you hadn't heard for forty years. Mary said to me, 'It's the most beautiful game in the world, played in this spirit.'

"My brother played a match on tour in Devon in about '46 or '47 and, when he went in, the umpire asked him if he wanted a trial ball. Ridiculous, isn't it? And he had one. Mind you, it did him no good. The bowler cleaned him up inside the over."

Cheltenham 1999. The left-handed Philip Weston plays across the line of the ball and is hit on the pads. For all his talking, Bomber's eyes have never left the game. "Ooowzzaat," the bowler roars, his appeal echoing off the college buildings, but the umpire gives a twitching shake of his head. "Terrible shot," Bomber says. "In my day that would have been out. The umpires looked after the game, you see. They didn't let people play shots like that."

"Who was here in 1947 then?" I ask, and for a moment the grief of all Gloucestershire brings our enthusiastic conversation to a halt.

August 1947. Gloucestershire versus Middlesex, first place against second, competing for a championship that Gloucestershire had never won, not since the competition was started properly in 1890. Not in Hammond's heyday, not even in the year of Bomber's birth, 1930, when the strangest of point-scoring systems gave Lancashire the title with 10 victories when Gloucestershire had won 15.

"I was in the army in the Middle East," Tom Graveney tells. "I was on the troop ship on the way home on leave. We listened to the commentary on the radio."

"I was here," Charles Light says. "It was very hot on the Saturday. We were living in Trull, and I cycled over. That would be 11 miles to Cirencester, then 15 from Cirencester to Cheltenham."

"That's a long journey on your day off work."

His son John smiles. "You should have heard my mother talking about the day they cycled to Gloucester. They got married in August 1938 and within the month he took his new bride down on push bikes from Sheepscombe to Gloucester to watch Hammond. To get home, you had to push your bike all up the hill to Painswick."

"She thought it was never-ending," Charles explains. "Well, of course, it is a long walk. But then we'd missed the cricket at Cheltenham that year."

"And did Hammond get runs?"

"I don't know," John says. "All I heard from Mum was what a long way it was to push the bike uphill."

I find the scorecard - *Hammond, lbw Cornford, 116* - and Charles inspects it. "Look at that. Emmett, 88, and he's batting at number seven."

"After the War," Bomber says, "when Wally was captain, he put all these lists up - what to do on Tuesday, Wednesday, Thursday - and Emmett said to the rest of the chaps, looking at the board, 'It's like being in the bloody army again.' He didn't know the great man was standing behind him. He said, 'I don't know what you're complaining about, Emmett, you're lucky to have your name on the board at all.' He didn't rate him."

"He picked Alfie Wilcox in front of him," Tom Graveney says, "which was the biggest joke of all time. Alfie was a lovely chap, but he was only a club player."

Here at Cheltenham in 1999 Graeme Hick is at the crease, and the runs are starting to flow. *'On a decent pitch of no great pace, with short boundaries square of the wicket, he gorged himself like a truffle-hunting porker.'*

"Here in 1947," Charles Light recalls, "the crowd at long-on was on the field, sitting inside the boundary, fifteen yards in."

"It's a nice crowd today," Bomber says, looking round the ground as Graeme Hick and Philip Weston take the score past 100, "but all the people here, there must have been as many as that locked outside."

The Gloucestershire Echo confirms their memories. *'Fifty motor coach loads of Middlesex supporters are expected. ... By 9.15 there were so many waiting that it was decided to open the gates an hour early. ... The heat was intense ... The gates were closed at 12.15 ... By lunch in some parts spectators had encroached 30 feet beyond the boundary line.'* The late Sam Cook was playing that day, and his daughter Carol treasures a few hand-written pages of his memories. 'A building firm was working at the College, and they were selling their empty paint tins to people who were standing at the back.'

The members' stand at the Middlesex match in 1947. George Emmett's wife Kathleen is looking to her right in the middle of the front row.

Middlesex began well. Bill Edrich, playing here because he was unfit to bowl in the Oval Test, hit a bright fifty, and it was 65 for one before B.O. Allen turned to Tom Goddard's off-spin. "Old Goddard," as the post-war players call him. He was 47 that year, and he took 238 wickets in the summer. Old Goddard, he wrapped his long index finger round the ball. In the words of John Arlott, *'When a ball from Tom Goddard struck a batsman's pads it was like an imperious rap at a door, and his appeal was a masterpiece of savagery.'* He took seven for 70, and the Middlesex innings subsided. *'The normal quiet of the College ground was punctuated with roars, as one Middlesex batsman after another trooped back to the pavilion.'* 180 all out, but Gloucester soon fared worse with 153. George Emmett top scorer, lbw to Jack Young for 33.

"Jack Young used to stay with us when he came to Cheltenham," George Emmett's daughter Gill recalls. "We lived in the Old Bath Road, and we had a Kerry blue terrier. The dog would let him in, he'd sit down, and it would sit in front of him. Then, as soon as he tried to move, it would growl. It didn't do it to anybody else."

Before close of play Edrich's pad received the imperious rap, the savage appeal met with success and, in Bill Edrich's own words, "I walked indoors while the ground shook with the deep-chested shouting of Gloucestershire farmers, who felt that I was but the first sheaf of a harvest." In came Harry Sharp in only his second championship match, promoted in the order to see them to close of play. For fifty years after the war he worked at Lord's, as player, coach, umpire and scorer, one of cricket's most popular characters, but it all might not have happened if the events of that evening had been different. John Light is a guide at Lord's now and, before Harry died, he told John the story. "I was playing for my place. I wasn't sure I was going to make it as a cricketer, and I got sent in as night-watchman. As soon as I got in, Goddard moved his slip to leg slip. I got an edge that first slip would have eaten. It was an absolute dolly, but it ran away for four, and in that moment my life was made."

"All through the weekend," Bill Edrich wrote, "there was an atmosphere of repressed excitement, throughout the hotel and in the staid and respectable streets of Cheltenham itself." Middlesex's George Mann relieved the tension at Sunday breakfast by recounting his dream, in which Tom Goddard's spinning finger had become one of the Devil's horns.

On Monday the ground grew even fuller: fifteen thousand, according to the Echo. Harry Sharp and Walter Robins added 70 for the third wicket, the Devil's horn took eight for 86, and Gloucestershire were left 169 to win. Gill Emmett and her Auntie Joyce walked to the ground. "My aunt had left something at home so we had to go back. So we decided not to wait for the bus. We went over the old railway line. We must have been a mile and a half from the ground when we started hearing the cheering. Every run was being applauded."

The groans came as well, though, and Gloucestershire were all out for 100. Old Tom Goddard the last victim, caught Edrich bowled Young, 0. Young Sam Cook, not out, 0. 1947 will always be remembered for Middlesex's great batsmen, the Brylcreem Summer of Compton and Edrich. Only the folk of Gloucestershire know how nearly it was the summer of Goddard and Cook. More than fifty years have passed, and the county is still waiting for that first championship title.

"We were bitterly disappointed," Gill Emmett says, "but the Cheltenham Festival was just one big party."

"Tom Goddard went home and cried," Sam Cook's memoir reads. "I went home and got drunk."

"It was a golden match to remember," Bill Edrich wrote, but the Gloucestershire memories now dwell only on that wonderful moment in the Middlesex second innings when Walter Robins hit old Goddard towards the crowd in front of the hospital. Cliff Monks, fielding at long-on ran twenty, thirty, who knows how many yards around the boundary *and caught the ball right-handed, waist high from the ground.*' "He ran like a hare," Bill Edrich wrote, "and he caught it with one hand outstretched high up among the crowd." The crowd were all over the outfield, and he plucked it almost from their midst: "I was right there," Bomber tells. "It would have hit me on the head." But the Guardian's Frank Keating says the same and, he writes, "I've heard more than a dozen men claim that over the years." "Cor! The crowd went mad," Bomber adds. "Even Robins stood in the middle of the wicket, clapping his bat."

Cliff Monks played 65 times for Gloucestershire, but over half his 16-line obituary in Wisden is devoted to this one catch.

Middlesex, 180 and 141. Gloucestershire, 153 and 100. A three-day match all over in two. Today the marketing men would shake their heads. But what did the captains say afterwards to the Echo?

B.O. Allen of Gloucestershire: "Cricket is a much better game on a wicket where the bowler has a fair chance than on a pitch on which the bowler's only hope is for the batsman to make a mistake."

R.W.V. Robins of Middlesex, a Test selector: "We want to develop and encourage spin bowlers in this country, and this is just the type of wicket we need."

August 1947. "That was the year they introduced the Agricultural Workers' Wages Act," John Light tells and, at the end of the month, the minimum wage for adult male land workers was increased by ten shillings to four pounds ten. For a 48-hour week. "For Cotswold working people, your holiday before then was to go to the cricket at Cheltenham."

The cricket at Cheltenham. Here in 1999 the score approaches 250, and Graeme Hick completes his 106th first-class century. Hard on a day like this to fathom how he is again out of the England team.

"If you were Chairman of Selectors, Bomber, instead of David Graveney, would you pick him?"

"I said to David, 'If you've got any sense between your ears, you should tell Hick he'll play if he bowls. And if he doesn't want to bowl, you'll bugger him off. He'll never be a great player, but he's the best all-rounder we've got.' I told him that years ago."

"I sometimes wonder if he'll be the Tom Graveney of this generation. He'll come back in, score a pack of runs, and everybody will wonder why he wasn't playing all along."

"That's exactly what I've said to him," Tom says. "'You're only 32. You haven't started yet.' I found as a batsman that the longer I went on the better I got."

Gloucestershire have turned to their eighth bowler, and Hick swings the ball high over the roof of the gymnasium and into the road. For several minutes there is no cricket, then the umpires produce a box of replacement balls.

"What was the most memorable match you played here, Bomber?"

"Cooky's benefit," he answers. "Against Yorkshire. An amazing match."

"Was that the one," Tom Graveney asks, "when we all had to come out …?"

"Yes, that's the one."

"I saw that," Charles Light says. "The first day and the last. Gloucester didn't want all that many to win, did they?"

"It only lasted two days."

Another spinner's wicket. Another match that they all remember.

Maybe we can tell the story of this one.

"Would you like another cup of tea?"

"No, it's all right, thank you, Bomber."

"Mary, pour Stephen another cup of tea."

Tom Graveney

ALL SHOOK UP

The summer of 1957

It is the second summer of commercial television. *'A new force has emerged throughout the country,'* the advertisement reads, *'shaping people's tastes, keeping them informed, moulding new patterns of behaviour. Ten years ago there were barely 15,000 television sets in Britain. Today the rooftop aerials tell a very different story. There are now over seven million sets in use.'*

Saturday the 17th of August. Gloucestershire viewers can turn their dials to five for the Wenvoe transmitter and pick up the BBC from three in the afternoon. Swimming and Motorcycling. The Lone Ranger. Billy Bunter. The Six-Five Special. Wells Fargo. The Jimmy Wheeler Show. Wilfred Pickles Tells a Story. The News and Weather, then the Close Down at eleven.

The first detector vans are at work, and plans are under way for the Queen to televise her Christmas message. To counter falling radio audiences, the Light Programme is starting two hours earlier now at seven o'clock, and 'trailers' are introduced, *'whereby listeners are told of other items to follow'*. The Home Service broadcasts 'Hancock's Half Hour', the Light Programme 'Summer Airs', in which 'Brian Johnston goes in search of holiday-makers who will challenge Gerald Shaw at the BBC theatre organ to play their favourite tunes.'

The summer of 1957. There are no motorways yet, but there are five million cars on the roads. The AA recruits its two millionth member, the Metropolitan Police tow away their first vehicles, and a motorist is convicted of speeding on the evidence of radar. Meanwhile, British Rail announces a loss of £16 million.

There are six million telephones, the first £1,000 premium bond prizes are drawn by ERNIE, and the Spanish village of Benidorm is the talk of the holiday trade. *'New hotels are going up everywhere,'* one reporter writes. *'The people are charming, not yet spoilt by easy money.'*

The minimum weekly wage for an agricultural worker rises to £7 - 10s. The maximum for a footballer goes up to £17, with a £4 win bonus and £2 extra for appearing in televised matches. The Confederation of Shipbuilding and Engineering Unions demands sick pay, transferable pensions, a 44-hour week and a third week's paid holiday.

The summer of 1957. Harold Macmillan, the new Prime Minister, is shooting grouse on the Yorkshire Moors. His government is still recovering from the Suez Crisis, and a Gallup Poll gives a 19-point lead to Hugh Gaitskell's Labour Party. In July Macmillan rallies the party faithful in Bedford: "Let us be frank about it: most of our people have never had it so good. Go around the country, go to the industrial towns, go to the farms, and you will see a state of prosperity such as we have never had in my life - nor indeed ever in the history of this country."

The summer of 1957. The Common Market Treaty is ratified, and the British Gold Coast becomes the independent republic of Ghana. Three hundred new cases of polio are reported each week, there is concern over the growing use of tranquillisers, and the Wolfenden Report recommends liberalising the law on homosexuality. The Medical Council finds 'direct cause and effect' in the relationship between smoking and lung cancer, and a BMA meeting debates: 'Is it cancer? Should a doctor tell?'

There are plans to put pictures of beauty spots on the postage stamps, and a Times editorial makes its opinion clear. *'Have we not for generations looked down on small countries that had to resort to such devices? The Postmaster General is the head of a great Government Department, not of a fancy goods store.'*

John Gielgud plays Prospero at Stratford, while at the Royal Court Laurence Olivier is Archie Rice in John Osborne's 'The Entertainer'. In the cinema Alec Guinness stars in 'The Bridge on the River Kwai', and the Edinburgh Festival opens with the Boulting Brothers' 'Lucky Jim': *'It provoked an almost endless ripple of comfortable laughter.'* The Festival also features an exhibition of paintings by Monet. *'He has long been in critical disfavour,'* the Times notes. *'The time is ripe for a revaluation.'*

August the seventeenth, 1957. Buy a copy of the New Musical Express, turn to the Hit Parade on page five and you will find Elvis Presley with his first number one, 'All Shook Up'.

'My head is shaking, and my knees are weak,
I can't seem to stand on my own two feet …
I'm in love, I'm all shook up.'

Alongside this the sheet music chart is headed by 'Around The World':

'No more will I go all around the world
For I have found my world in you.'

In September there will be a new number one on the Hit Parade: 'Diana' by Paul Anka. Then in November it will be 'That'll Be The Day' by Buddy Holly and the Crickets, as a new rock'n'roll generation takes over.

"We had this chap at Bristol," Bomber says. "Geoff Mains. He was a flashy dresser. Whatever came along, he had to wear it. He came in one day in this real teddy boy outfit: powder blue suit, hair quiffed up, crepe shoes. Colonel Henson was the secretary. 'Good God, what's that?' he said. 'That's the vogue these days, Colonel,' I said. And he shouted across: 'Don't you dare go in that pavilion, Mains, dressed like that.' He sent him home to change."

'Three Teddy Boys Arrested,' is the Stroud News and Journal headline, reporting a fight at a Friday night dance. *'The incidents began after the arrival of a party of 30 to 40 Gloucester Teddy boys, who had travelled by rail car.'* The years of austerity are over, and recorded crime is rising.

A calmer evening can be had at the Gaumont Theatre, Cheltenham, with 'glamorous Radio, TV and Recording Personality Alma Cogan. Plenty of good seats at 5/-, 4/-, 3/6 and 2/6.'

Twelve miles to the east, in Bourton-on-the-Water, there is controversy over the arrival of *'a rash of slot machines, selling bubble gum, sweets, black-and-yellow roll film, postcards, cigarettes and soft drinks.'* The Times reporter attempts to convey an idea of these strange contraptions: *'Pride of place went to an elaborate structure of revolving shelves, which displayed a range of souvenirs, leather, metal and pot, any of which could be released by the insertion of a florin.'*

The summer of 1957. In the F.A. Cup Final an injury to goal-keeper Ray Wood costs Manchester United's 'Busby Babes' the first League and Cup Double since 1893. Alf Ramsay's Ipswich are promoted to Division One, and in August a 17-year-old Jimmy Greaves makes his debut for Chelsea.

Lew Hoad wins the Wimbledon Men's Singles, and in the Ladies' event Althea Gibson becomes tennis's first black champion. Huddersfield's Doug Ibbotson takes the mile record down to 3 minutes 57.2 seconds, and Stirling Moss wins the British and Italian Grands Prix: *'I proved that a British car with a British driver can beat the lot.'*

In cricket England beat the visiting West Indians by three Tests to nil and, if there were a Wisden World Championship Table like the one they will introduce forty years later, it would show England clearly in first place:

		Series played	*Won*	*Lost*	*Drawn*	*Points*	*Average*
1.	England	10	6	0	4	16	1.60
2.	South Africa	5	2	1	2	6	1.20
2.	Pakistan	5	2	1	2	6	1.20
4.	Australia	7	3	3	1	7	1.00
5.	India	7	2	3	2	6	0.86
6.	West Indies	6	2	3	1	5	0.83
7.	New Zealand	6	0	6	0	0	0.00

Saturday the 17th of August, 1957. The morning papers all tell of Surrey's sixth successive championship title, secured at Weston-super-Mare yesterday evening: *'Laker was ready with a dab to third man seven minutes from time, and so Surrey retired to brief celebrations on rose-petal wine after which it only remained for May to pay tribute to a gallant foe while parents held up their children to see the leader of a great side.'*

Six in a row. *'The hat-trick has been brought off several times,'* the Times writes, *'but a whole over's worth is unique.'*

'They are a good fighting team,' the Yorkshire Post adds, *'who have set up a veritable Everest of a record. Surrey, proud, valiant Surrey will yield up the championship one of these days. May it be Yorkshire who wrest it from them!'*

Down in Gloucestershire the Echo finds a local angle with a story about their county captain from the '30s: *'Bev Lyon admits he had an accumulator bet on Surrey. His initial stake is said to have been £5, and last year bookmakers are thought to have offered a settlement in advance, something in the region of £30,000. 'Yes, there was a bet,' he says. 'It was weighed and paid before the present season started.' Surrey are one of the few teams who can get other sides out twice in three days.''*

And his own county? What are their prospects? *'Gloucestershire are just not championship minded.'*

Surrey have bowlers who can get other sides out twice in three days, and the latest national averages have Lock, Loader, Laker and Bedser all in the first six. 'Ah, the Oval pitches,' they say around the country, but on these same pitches May, Barrington and Stewart have all made the batting averages. Peter May is at the head, too, fifteen runs an innings ahead of Tom Graveney in second place. For many, this Surrey side is the greatest county team of all time.

1957 sees the swan song of Denis Compton. Back in the summer of 1947 he brightened the hearts of a struggling post-war Britain with 3,816 sparkling, joyful runs. In the words of Neville Cardus, *'Compton spread his happy favours everywhere. The crowd sat in the sun, liberated from anxiety and privation.'* He is 39 now, restricted by his damaged knee, and he is on his last round of the county circuit, with three last centuries, one of them in Dickie Dodds' benefit match at Leyton.

Dickie is a committed Christian. He does not play on Sundays and, unlike most professionals, he does not insure his benefit match against rain. Instead, he prays to his God, and he is blessed with glorious sunshine and East London's last glimpse of Denis. "He did not disappoint them," Dickie writes. "He made a magnificent century, with some superb shots. I still remember one. He ran down the wicket and seemed to be aiming to hit the ball for six over mid-off. At the last moment he turned the angle of his bat and hit it over mid-on instead." Dickie's benefit raises £2,325, and he gives it all to Moral Re-Armament.

Cricket in the summer of 1957. The county championship is a vibrant competition with large crowds at Chesterfield and Leyton, at Cheltenham and Weston-super-Mare, and its title is won eight days before the start of the football season. BBC radio introduces ball-by-ball commentary from the Tests, and at Edgbaston England's two greatest batsmen add 411 for the fourth wicket to snuff out the mystery of Sonny Ramadhin's spin.

Peter May, 285 not out. Colin Cowdrey, 154. I listen to it on the radio when I get home from school. Then in July I have my appendix out. 'Do you like cricket?' the surgeon asks me, as he prepares the anaesthetic. 'You do? Well, I'll bowl you an over.' He stands above me, imitating John Arlott, and by the fourth ball I am far away.

Every boy knows the names: May and Cowdrey, Laker and Lock, Trueman and Statham, Bailey and Graveney. Cricket is England's summer game.

We have never had it so good. But Harold Macmillan's speech continues: 'What is beginning to worry some of us is, is it too good to be true? - or perhaps I should say, is it too good to last?'

Tom Graveney is twelfth man at Edgbaston. "Colin kicked Ram to death," he says. This is the old lbw law, when you cannot be given out if the pad is outside the off-stump. "It broke poor Ram's heart. You should have seen him in the hotel. 'He got 154,' he said, 'but I had him lbw 89 times.' The West Indies asked him to tour in '63, but he didn't want to play."

The law changes in 1970. The batsman can be lbw outside the off-stump if he is not playing a shot.

"They pretend they're using the bat when they're not," Tom says. "If I was an umpire, I'd say, 'You've got one more chance. You do that again and it's hitting the stumps, you're out.'"

"Ramadhin," Bomber glows. "Such a wonderful bowler to watch!"

Colin Cowdrey is a wonderful batsman, too, and Bomber recalls him at Cheltenham the previous summer. "I got my hundredth wicket when I caught and bowled him, but he got runs in the second innings on a brute of a wicket. He was all spattered with mud from where the ball reared up and hit him. A masterly display. Emrys Davies was umpiring at my end, and he turned to me. 'He's a good 'un,' he said, 'a bloody good 'un. Long may he reign.'" But Bomber recalls Colin's pad play that day as well. "I must have had him lbw twenty times. I can see now George Emmett and Arthur Milton staring at the spot where the ball was pitching and looking down the wicket to Emrys. But Colin was an amateur, and the amateur carried great sway. And if the umpire didn't give an amateur out, the professional at the other end knew he'd better be careful."

The summer of 1957. Just four counties have professional captains, and the M.C.C. sets up a sub-committee under the chairmanship of the Duke of Norfolk to look at the status of the amateurs.

This year's cricketing autobiographies are all by the slow men - Wardle, Laker and Lock - but then last summer was their high water mark: nineteen wickets for Jim Laker at Old Trafford and, of the 23 bowlers to take 100 wickets, 17 were spinners. By 1962, it will be just four out of 23: three off-spinners and Tony Lock's slow left arm.

Cricket is changing, and in 1957 a quartet of leg-spinners all take their last championship wickets: Doug Wright and Eric Hollies, Roly Jenkins and the Australian Bruce Dooland. Just eight years back, there were three leg-spinners in the England side. Soon there will not be three on the whole county circuit.

At the end of the year Gloucestershire will present their annual accounts. In 1955 they lost £416. In 1956 it was £1,769. Now it is £5,394. The motor cars, the television sets, the rock'n'roll, the hotels in Benidorm. They are all novelties, but their effects are already starting to be felt.

There is a Political and Economic Planning report on 'The Cricket Industry', and it tries to find hope amid this gathering gloom: *'In crudely economic terms, county cricket is fighting a losing battle. But, as anyone who has ever tried to explain cricket to a foreigner knows, logic has no part in it. Along with the English licensing laws, early closing, driving on the left and British weights and measures, it may well survive and confound all its critics.'*

Forty years have passed, and we still drive on the left.

Let's sit down and enjoy ourselves in 1957. And what better a place to be than at Cheltenham for Sam Cook's benefit match.

DAMP AND GREEN

The morning of the first day

Saturday morning. At the bus stop in King's Square, Gloucester, Bomber is standing in his sports coat and flannels. "You weren't allowed to wear your blazer away from the ground." He is waiting for the Bristol Tramways bus. An eight-mile, 45-minute journey through Staverton to Cheltenham. "It was packed, but people would stand aside. 'Come on, Bomb, get on.' I'd put my leather bag in the hold, sit upstairs and have a natter with all the folk going to the game. "'What's the pitch going to do, Bomber?' ... 'Are we going to beat them?' ... 'If I were George Emmett,' they'd say, 'I'd bring in Etheridge.' Or 'I'd put a man deeper at square leg for Cooky.' And I used to agree with them, never disagree. It was wonderful to listen to all their ideas.

"Spectators see a different game from what the players see. I learnt that. But now I think the professionals disregard the public. They're of no consequence."

Saturday morning. Gloucestershire's captain George Emmett and his wife are driving up from Bristol. They moved down from their rented maisonette in Cheltenham when he became the county coach, and he used his benefit money to buy a house in Sea Mills. "He had an old sit-up-and-beg Ford Anglia," his daughter Gill tells. George is 44 years old, a veteran of the Desert campaign and the Sicily landings, and he is not one to tolerate indiscipline. "The number plate was GAD 18, and some of them used to make comments about George and the Dragon. My mother was less than impressed."

In the back seat of the Anglia is his Kerry blue terrier. "Looking back," she says. "I'm surprised that dog survived all day sitting in the car." Bomber laughs: "We'd walk past the car deliberately, and of course the dog would go mad."

"Colonel Henson was the Secretary," Gill tells. "A nice old man. Terribly, terribly pukka. He had a Rolls, and for some reason - he must have been very absent-minded - he opened the door of Dad's car. I don't know how you can mistake an Anglia for a Rolls, no matter how deep in thought you are. And the dog hurtled out, pushed him back against his own car. 'George,' he shouted."

"Cheltenham was the Mecca," Bomber recalls. "People from all over the county came, and the hotels were booked up with people taking their holidays. To get a good view, you had to get there an hour before the start. And you saw Colonel Henson walking round in his country dress: Harris tweed jacket, cavalry twill trousers, brown shoes, county tie. There were boys all round the boundary, but they were as good as gold. They rarely came onto the field. They'd have been frightened to death of Colonel Henson. He just kept walking round the ground, and he always looked immaculate."

Times are changing, though, and 1957 is the first year in office of the new Secretary, Harold Thomas. "He was a gentleman," Bomber says. "A lovely chap, but he wasn't like the Colonel. He wouldn't say boo to a dicky bird."

Saturday morning. Sam Cook stands outside the front door of his council house in Shipton Moyne, two miles south of Tetbury. He has promised his wife Daisy that they will have a bungalow built with his benefit money, and anxiously he looks up at the sky.

CECIL COOK

'One of the wettest Augusts for years in Cheltenham,' the Echo reports. To the west, the river Severn is nine feet above normal, and Tewkesbury has been flooded. So damp was the College wicket for the Hampshire match that play started at 2.30 on Wednesday and was all over on Thursday. *'Two days,'* the Echo reckons, *'are enough to finish any match at the College.'*

Cecil Cook. Everybody calls him Sam, though no one knows why. A county cricketer for the last twelve summers, he is a plumber in winter, a cheerful Cotswold man who likes his beer and his cricket. He has an England blazer from his one Test in 1947, and he features this summer in the cards issued with Adventure comics.

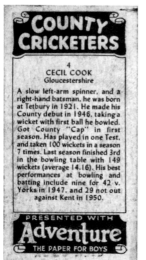

These are anxious hours for Sam, but at least the sun is bright as Daisy and the two girls climb into his car. "A little black Austin," Carol the older one recalls, "with those clonking yellow indicators." Slowly they climb up Painswick Hill, past the yew trees in the churchyard, and soon they are looking down on the town of Cheltenham.

"He was driving for years before he took his test," Bomber recalls. "The constabulary knew, but they never stopped him." For Sam this car has made a world of difference to his cricketing life, and Carol shows me the hand-written pages that form the start of his memoir. 'Bowling Down The Road', it is called, and he tells how in his early days Charlie Barnett picked him up each morning on his way through Tetbury. "At the end of the month, he said to me, 'How much is your bus fare?' It was four and sixpence. 'In that case, you owe me twelve four and sixpences.'"

Then at the end of 1948 Charlie Barnett retired. "So I became the Hitch-Hiking Cricketer." Waiting for the Bristol bus at seven each morning, bowling 30 or 40 overs in the day, then hoping that somebody would respond to Colonel Henson's message over the tannoy. "If anybody is going to Tetbury, Sam Cook would like a lift home." It is a charming story, but his memoir tells of the many days when there is no response and Sam has to take the bus to Malmesbury and walk five miles home. "If we were playing at Cheltenham I had to get off at Kingscote, and that was seven miles."

He has worked hard to buy this car, and soon he will have his own house, too.

"There were certain matches you couldn't choose for your benefit," Bomber recalls. "The tourist match and the Bank Holiday game against Somerset. Versus Yorkshire at Cheltenham, he did well to get that one. That would have been quite a concession."

It is almost fifty years since Yorkshire have come to Cheltenham, and one old Gloucestershire member can recall the delight of Colonel Henson the previous summer. "He was a very military gentleman, and he was talking to a lady as I passed by. 'I've got Yorkshire coming next year,' he said. It was a major achievement."

Surrey may have won their sixth championship yesterday evening, but Yorkshire still draw the crowds wherever they go. England's largest county with a great cricketing tradition and so many household names: Freddie Trueman and Johnny Wardle, Willie Watson and Brian Close. "To us Cotswolds lads," John Light explains, "they were like a visiting Test team from a distant Northern kingdom. They came from a different world."

Saturday morning. John parks his bike at the Swan in Cirencester and boards the bus. "There was a lad from Swindon, Howlett. He never got a first-class game. They used to make him twelfth man at Cheltenham because it was cheaper to pay his bus fares, and the buses were regular. I would travel back to Cirencester with him."

No. That story belongs in a future year. Today the eleventh place lies between David Allen and Bomber: both off-spinners in a twelve that also includes a third, John Mortimore, and the slow left-arm of Sam Cook himself. According to the Echo, Bomber is *'a firm favourite with the Cheltenham crowd'*, and a cheer goes up when his name is announced on the loudspeaker. "I think I came back by demand," he laughs. "Maybe they thought it would put a few more on the gate. Who knows? Cooky may have asked for me to play."

A nice idea, but the explanation probably lies with the change of wicket-keeper. Peter Rochford has gone home ill, and Bobby Etheridge is taking his place. David Allen has played the first two matches of the Festival but only as a batsman. With Etheridge adding to the batting, there is room once more for Bomber. Even in 1957, it seems, a tail of Rochford, Cook and Wells is better avoided.

"A year or two before that," their team mate Tony Brown recalls, "they had Frank McHugh as well. People used to say, 'There's a hat-trick in there for any decent bowler.' Apparently there was one game when two of them were on as runners for the other two, and all four of them finished up at the same end." The career averages in the 1957 News Chronicle Annual read: Wells 6.64, Rochford 5.60, Cook 5.03, McHugh 2.63.

David Allen. It is easy with hindsight to fetch down Wisden and see his 122 Test wickets. Of English off-spinners, only Laker, Titmus and Emburey stand above him. But in 1957 his path into this Gloucestershire side is blocked by John Mortimore and Bomber. Five summers he has been trying to establish himself, and next year he will not play here at all. Then in 1959, with Tom Graveney as captain offering him a regular place, the Cheltenham crowd will cheer the news of his selection for the Oval Test. "I went to the committee at the end of 1958," he tells. "I didn't want to spend ten or twelve years in the game and leave with nothing, having done nothing. 'They're bad judges of me,' I was thinking. 'I want to go.'"

"They asked me what I thought of him," Bomber says. "If I'd said he wasn't good enough, I think he'd have been on his way." So Bomber spends 1959 in the second eleven. "George Emmett was captain of the seconds by then, but he got called back to the first team and I had to take over. He hardly played." Bomber takes 87 wickets in 12 games, nobody else in the country passes 60, and they win the new Second Eleven Championship. "If you want to catch people out," he says, "ask them who's the only captain who's ever won a championship for Gloucestershire." Alas, Wisden won't confirm Bomber's answer: *'They owed much to George Emmett, their captain,'* it records.

Here in 1957 Peter Rochford has gone home to Halifax. He is feeling ill, and he has made his last appearance in first-class cricket. Let's leave it at that. "He should have played for England," Bomber says. "He was so neat. He'd stump someone with just a flick of the bail." "At his best," Tom Graveney says, "he was brilliant. But he wasn't always at his best."

Alan Gibson's All-Time Gloucestershire Eleven - captain, W.G. Grace - has Rochford at number nine, between Procter and Parker. "I have never seen anyone with a more natural talent for the job, and therefore I picked him at his brief best, hoping that W.G. would manage to keep him in order."

Today Bobby Etheridge replaces him, released by Bristol City from their pre-season friendly at Ashton Gate. "Eth," Bomber smiles. "He counted every run he scored, no matter what the match was. We played at Leicester in the seconds, he had 99 on the board, and he pushed this single. They all clapped, but he never recognised it. Alec Skelding the old umpire was scoring. 'He's an ungrateful bugger,' he said to me. 'You've probably got the score wrong,' I said and, sure enough, he got another single and waved his bat in the air.

"Eth came from Gloucester like me. In fact he must be the greatest all-round sportsman the city's ever had. Cricket for the county, football for Bristol City. He played bowls for Gloucestershire as well."

"He was a natural games player," Tony Brown adds. "He had a wonderful eye, and he was a great striker of the ball. But he was always rather unkempt, and his keeping could be a bit untidy."

George Emmett's Kerry blue terrier sits alone in the Ford Anglia, Bomber arrives from the Bristol Tramways bus, and Sam Cook's family meet up with the other wives and children. But, alas, *'the sun was bright too early. By the time Yorkshire got to their dressing room the sky was full of cloud and, before they had completed their bit of pre-match practice, the rain was coming straight down.'* The covers are rushed out - for the match has not started - and the players look for other amusements.

First, there are the card games. "In my early days, when we travelled by train," Tom Graveney recalls, "we had two tables of Auction Bridge. Monty

Cranfield used to get the best hands all the time. He was the luckiest card player I ever met, and Tom Goddard wasn't a good loser. If he played against Cranny, he ended up throwing the cards out of the window."

Monty has gone, and Arthur Milton is now the man to beat. Bomber laughs: "Jack Crapp said to me, 'Never play cards against Milt. You haven't got a chance. He'll read your mind.' Every game he played he'd beat you. Darts, billiards, snooker, table tennis. He had this little rubber ball in his bag. We had to bounce it across the table. The trick was to get it to nick the edge. You'd play up to five or ten. He was even unbeatable at that."

Arthur Milton. The last man to play both cricket and football for England.

"Everything he did, he did so easily," Tom Graveney says. "We took him up to this nine-hole golf course at Taunton one Sunday, and he took to it like a duck to water. Twelve months later, he was playing off four."

Are the cards out? Has Arthur produced his rubber ball? Sam Cook's spirits lift as *'the wait was not a long one.'* The start is only ten minutes late, and it falls to Sam to spin the coin. Billy Sutcliffe, the Yorkshire captain, calls correctly and decides to bat.

'The pitch was very green and was still damp,' the Gloucester Citizen reports, *'and Sutcliffe must have had second thoughts about his decision to bat.'*

Perhaps, it is time to check the scorecard. It's cost us fourpence.

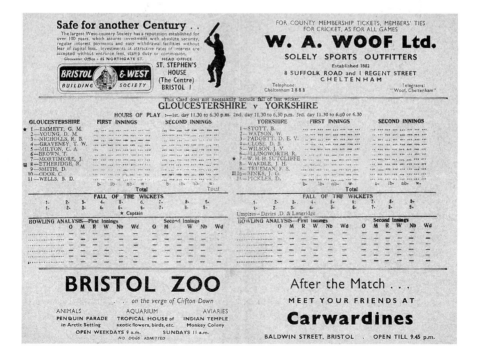

This Card does not necessarily include fall of last wicket.

GLOUCESTERSHIRE v YORKSHIRE

HOURS OF PLAY :—1st. day 11.30 to 6.30 p.m. 2nd. day 11.30 to 6.30 p.m. 3rd. day 11.30 to 6.00 or 6.30

GLOUCESTERSHIRE	FIRST INNINGS	SECOND INNINGS	YORKSHIRE	FIRST INNINGS	SECOND INNINGS
★ 1—EMMETT, G. M.			1—STOTT, B.		
2—YOUNG, D. M.			2—WATSON, W.		
3—NICHOLLS, R. B.			3—PADGETT, D. E. V.		
4—GRAVENEY, T. W.			4—CLOSE, D. B.		
5—MILTON, C. A.			5—WILSON, J. V.		
6—BROWN, T.			6—ILLINGWORTH, R.		
7—MORTIMORE, J.			★ 7—W. H. H. SUTCLIFFE		
☒ 8—ETHERIDGE, R.			8—WARDLE, J. H.		
9—SMITH, D.			9—TRUEMAN, F. S.		
10—COOK, C.			☒ 10—BINKS, J. G.		
11—WELLS, B. D.			11—PICKLES, D.		
b- lb- nb- w-	Total		b- lb- nb- w-	Total	

★ Captain

FALL OF THE WICKETS								
1-	2-	3-	4-	5-	6-	7-	8-	9-
1-	2-	3-	4-	5-	6-	7-	8-	9-

Umpires—Davies ,D. & Langridge

FALL OF THE WICKETS								
1-	2-	3-	4-	5-	6-	7-	8-	9-
1-	2-	3-	4-	5-	6-	7-	8-	9-

BOWLING ANALYSIS—First Innings						Second Innings						BOWLING ANALYSIS—First Innings						Second Innings					
O	M	R	W	Nb	W	O	M		W	Nb	Wd	O	M	R	W	Nb	Wd	O	M	R	W	Nb	Wd

BRISTOL ZOO
. . on the verge of Clifton Down

ANIMALS	AQUARIUM	AVIARIES
PENGUIN PARADE	TROPICAL HOUSE of	INDIAN TEMPLE
in Arctic Setting	exotic flowers, birds, etc.	Monkey Colony

OPEN WEEKDAYS 9 a.m.   SUNDAYS 11 a.m.
NO DOGS ADMITTED

After the Match . . .

MEET YOUR FRIENDS AT

Carwardines

BALDWIN STREET, BRISTOL . OPEN TILL 9.45 p.m.

Who are the Yorkshire openers these days? Len Hutton has retired, Frank Lowson has been out injured most of the summer, so a new generation is seizing its opportunity. Last month, when Gloucestershire visited Scarborough, Yorkshire experimented with Ken Taylor and Bryan Stott, and already the bush telegraph of county cricket is chattering: stands of 122 and 230 at Trent Bridge, 115 at Hove, and with a dash that is very different from the days of Hutton and Lowson. "We had such a good understanding," Ken recalls. "We ran six singles in the first over at Old Trafford once. It wasn't what they expected in a Roses match."

Ken is back with Huddersfield Town, training for the coming football season, but he called in at Headingley on Tuesday so that Billy Sutcliffe could present him and Bryan with their county caps. Moving up to open in his place today is another footballer, Willie Watson, the last man before Arthur Milton to play both cricket and football for England. He will celebrate his 80th birthday in the year 2000, still in good health. "And he must have smoked a hundred cigarettes a day all his life," Ken Taylor adds.

Stott and Watson put on their pads, and the Gloucestershire team emerges, led as custom demands by Sam Cook. "Didn't he get a cheer?" Bomber laughs. "I think the old lad was rather embarrassed."

COOK LEADS OUT GLOUCESTERSHIRE. —Cook, who has chosen the match for his benefit, leads out the Gloucestershire side against Yorkshire in the Festival match at the College Ground today.

The picture on the front page of the Gloucestershire Echo

Saturday morning at Cheltenham. The wettest August for years. John Bapty is reporting the game for the Yorkshire Evening Post - "He was like one of those reporters in a Hollywood film," Ken Taylor recalls. "A little, round man, with shirtsleeves rolled up, smoking away." *'The wicket is so natural an affair,'* he writes, *'that it is not easy to pick it out from the rest of the ground.'*

"It was sandy soil," Tony Brown explains, "but, because of the slope, they always had terrible difficulty stopping the water getting onto the square. Flat sheet covers hadn't been invented so they put down sandbags or rolled-up blankets to stop the rain running under the covers. But it wasn't that efficient."

Jim Hammond, the old Sussex player, is the college's cricket professional, his wife runs the tuck shop, and in five years' time he will be succeeded by Lancashire's Geoff Edrich. "When I started there," Geoff says, "they were using the same covers they'd used when W.G. Grace played. And there wasn't the staff or the equipment that they have now. Vic Thornton was the Head Groundsman. I don't think he'd ever played cricket, and he didn't know much about the game." But did he know about preparing a wicket? "Oh, I wouldn't like to say that."

In the 1950s wickets are not covered during the course of the match, there is not the fertiliser or the imported loam, and there are many more out-grounds like this one here at Cheltenham. So the players are used to playing on all sorts of surfaces. "It made for far more interesting cricket," Geoff says.

More interesting cricket certainly but, for the beneficiary, there are not always three days of takings. In 1953 Lancashire travelled down to Bath for Bertie Buse's benefit match. "We walked across the square on Saturday morning," Geoff remembers. "The groundsman was there, and we looked down at the wicket. Honestly, it's not a story. You could see the squares on the wicket where it had been re-turfed, and they hadn't knitted together properly. 'What do you think of it, gentlemen?' he said. And I said to him, ever so politely, 'Monday lunchtime, at the latest.' 'Oh no, ' he said. 'They always play better than they look here.'

"Harold Gimblett came out to bat, and the first ball of the match pitched, and a piece of earth came out, half the size of the ball practically. There was the ball and this bit of earth coming at Harold, and he looked round at us. 'It's one of those rough days, gentlemen.' He didn't stay long."

Nobody did stay that day. The match was over by six o'clock, and only sympathy saved Bertie Buse from financial disaster. So it is not just the weather that worries Sam Cook as today's cricket gets under way.

J.M. Kilburn underlines the problem in the Yorkshire Post: *'The ball swung readily and came from the soft pitch at variable pace and height.'* With so much rain Yorkshire's batsmen have only been to the wicket once in the last ten days, and that too contributes to their problems: *'Yorkshire batted exactly as they might have batted in an April outdoor practice. They played too late, they played too soon; they followed the ball outside the off stump, they mistimed on the leg. In short, they were out of practice.'*

David Smith takes the first over for Gloucestershire. Early last summer he was a wiry young man in Bristol club cricket, a short-spell bowler with a touch of asthma, now he is nearing the end of a full season of county cricket, a season in which he will bowl over 900 overs. "He had the best natural action in England," David Allen says. Willie Watson pushes his fourth ball for a single, then to the fifth *'Stott played defensively at a ball that swerved and hit his off stump.'* It is Bryan Stott's first innings in a Yorkshire cap, and he is bowled first ball.

Stott, bowled Smith, 0   **Yorkshire, 1 for one**

Doug Padgett, at number three, is off the mark with an edged single through the slips, but soon *'Watson's brief innings ended. A ball from Smith was turned to short leg and there, of course, Milton made no mistake.'*

These are the days of uncovered wickets, with close catchers all round the bat, and there is not a pair of hands in the whole of England as quick and safe as those of Arthur Milton. Last summer he won the County Cup, with its hundred pound prize, for his 63 catches; not even the wicket-keepers took more. "He used to catch shots," Bomber says. "Not just mis-drives and bat-and-pad things. He'd just toss the ball back to the keeper. 'He'd catch even more,' old George Emmett said, 'if he wasn't scratching his nose halfway through each over.'"

How the game will change! In 1999 the leading keeper takes 67 catches, and there is not an out-fielder with more than 30.

Watson, caught Milton, bowled Smith, 3   **Yorkshire, 4 for two**

Brian Close appears next. His on-off Test career resumed at the start of the summer, but he is once more in the wilderness. England's youngest ever cricketer in 1949, he will appear in just 22 Tests in 28 years. He plays to win, and statistics, safety, career are all subordinated to his latest theory. "He sent Philip Sharpe and me out one day when he was captain," Ken Taylor recalls. "He was looking to set a target. 'I want 100 runs in 40 minutes,' he said. 'Don't get out, and don't make it look easy.'" "I remember batting with him at Taunton when he was well into his forties," Somerset's Peter Robinson tells. "Andy Roberts was the fastest bowler in the country, and Closey came down the wicket and let the ball hit him on the chest. 'What are you doing?' I asked. 'I just wanted to see how fast he was.'"

"If he'd had an ounce more grey matter," Bomber says, "he'd have been England captain for ten years. He was a bit puddled."

Here at Cheltenham he pulls a short ball for three, he hits a full toss for four, and on the soft pitch he tries to drive Tony Brown and is *'neatly caught at short mid-wicket'.*

Close, caught Mortimore, bowled Brown, 7   **Yorkshire, 15 for three**

Doug Padgett, with a square cut and an off-drive, hits two *'handsome'* fours, and Vic Wilson, *'who has had a sketchy time of late'*, scatters the close field with a four to square leg, *'a stroke of some merit on such a morning'*. But David Smith and Tony Brown are not done on this damp, green wicket, and by the time the first hour is complete they have *'run through the cream of the batting.'*

Padgett, caught Etheridge, bowled Brown, 18   **Yorkshire, 28 for four**
Wilson, caught Milton, bowled Smith, 8   **Yorkshire, 38 for five**

The scoreboard still shows 38 when Ray Illingworth edges a low off-side ball from Tony Brown. Behind the wicket Bobby Etheridge dives to his right, *'but the ball just failed to stick.'* According to the Yorkshire Post, *'the fielders were already acclaiming it.'*

"Rochy would have had that," some mutter in the crowd.

"On a good day," others reply.

Yorkshire's captain Billy Sutcliffe, *'who must have been deeply regretting his decision to bat'*, remains on nought for 25 minutes. *'So far was he out of touch that half a dozen times he missed the ball by at least the bat's width.'* But the two young bowlers are coming to the end of their spells. *'Had Emmett been able to call on a third fast bowler,'* the Times reckons, *'Yorkshire would probably have been back in the pavilion before lunch.'* Instead, he turns to his spinners - and the first of them, from the Chapel End, is Sam Cook.

Sam. Has he taken a moment to look round the boundary? *'There was not an empty seat in the ground now, the crowd having grown to over 5,000.'* They cheer his introduction. They applaud politely as Illingworth hits him for four and pulls Tony Brown into the main stand for six. They clap ironically when Sutcliffe finally gets off the mark. Then John Mortimore takes over from the College Lawn End, and Illingworth promptly sweeps him for another boundary.

According to the Yorkshire Post, the batsmen have *'conceived a happy division of labour: Sutcliffe brought all his resolution to comparatively passive defence while Illingworth went boldly into adventure.'* Ten minutes before lunch George Emmett turns to Bomber and again to David Smith, but the partnership, *'permitted by the initial fielding error'* by Etheridge, has by now turned into *'a superb exhibition of soft-wicket batsmanship.'*

"Ray was a hell of a good cricketer," Tom Graveney reckons.

"If Raymond had played with any other county," Fred Trueman says, "he'd have gone in number three or four and got two thousand runs easy."

"Illingworth batted beautifully," John Light recalls, a seventeen-year-old in the stands at the Chapel End. "I'd never seen him before. He played a splendid innings. Full of character and skill - and courage, too, because the ball was flying."

Illingworth, not out 37
Sutcliffe, not out 15   **Yorkshire, 88 for five**

It is time for lunch.

GROWING UP IN GLOUCESTER

Lunch on the first day

I pull out a cheese roll and an end of cucumber.

"Have some baby tomatoes," Bomber says. "Mary, have you got some tomatoes for Stephen?"

Politely I pick two from the large brown paper bag.

"Go on. That's not enough. Take some more. They're absolutely delicious. They're from the greenhouse. Mary, give him some more."

In marquees all round the ground the wine is starting to flow - though not for Bomber. He has been a teetotaller all his life.

"We used to lunch with the Mayor on the first day," Arthur Milton recalls. "I remember one occasion in my early days when George Lambert and Colin Scott were playing. We had some wine, and I think George had one or two glasses too many. He came up to bowl the first over after lunch, and he ran straight into the wickets."

"My first game there," Tom Graveney remembers, "was against Essex. The Mayor got up. 'It's nice to welcome the men from Exeter.' He went on, what a pity it was that neither side was any good. 'At least,' he said, 'we've got two up-and-coming young men, the brothers Gravity.'"

The Mayor's Reception at lunch on the first day. Bomber still recalls the occasion in 1954. Derbyshire 45 for no wicket at the break. "I was walking over with Les Jackson, and the Mayor, Charlie Irving, was outside the marquee, shaking hands with everyone. 'Typical Derbyshire,' he said. '45 for nought at lunch. No wonder people don't come to watch the game like they used to.' 'Steady on, Mister Mayor,' I said. 'They've already bowled us out for 43.'"

"You grew up in Gloucester, Bomber?"

"That's right."

'Gloucester,' Coleridge wrote, 'is a nothing-to-be-said-about town.' But then he never sat down with Bomber.

"So when did you first become aware of cricket?"

"You don't realise you're taking it in, do you? When you're young, you don't realise what you're storing away in your cranium.

"I can see them now, my dad and his brothers. Sitting around the coal fire and putting the cricket and rugby world to rights. Our dad sat there in his grandfather chair, flanked by my uncles. And there I was on the lino floor, listening.

"I listened to them talking about Charlie Parker, Wally Hammond, Tom Goddard, all those great Gloucestershire cricketers. My uncles would come round in the winter, and I would sit by the fire and visualise these great gods. Charlie Parker: if he couldn't bowl them out with his spinners, he could bowl them out with his seam. Wally Hammond, so brilliant he could play the ball with just the edge of his bat. Tom Goddard, he could spin it from one side of the pitch to the other.

"They'd sit there. All of them drank. They'd have a crate of beer on the table, a couple of dozen bottles, and they'd down the lot. And all the time they'd be talking about cricket. Picking their best England team, that sort of thing. And the more they had to drink, the more Gloucestershire players there'd be in the side. And I just listened. I never realised it, the actual effect it was having on me at the time.

"We lived at 69 New Street, Gloucester, my mum and dad and the four of us. They were just two-up, two-down terraced houses, no bathroom, the toilet outside, but there were families of ten or more crammed in those little houses. Everybody in Gloucester had heard of New Street. There'd been a horrendous murder there, some people called it Murder Alley, but it wasn't really a rough area. It was one of those streets where your parents could leave the rent money, the bread or the milk money, underneath the mat, and it was never ever stolen.

"The local factories were Morelands, the match-makers, Fielding and Platt the engineers, and the Wagon Works, where they made wagons and coaches for the railways. Most of the workers lived in the streets around us so they walked or cycled to work. The only vehicle down our street was the next-door neighbour's horse and cart. He used to go round, picking up the dustbins.

"My dad was an ardent socialist. He was a millwright by trade - millers, they used to call them - and he led the first strike at the Wagon Works. He was victimised afterwards, and he worked on the barges, anything to get a job. He had amazing principles. Quite often he'd go down the prison on a Sunday morning when they used to release the prisoners. He'd grab hold of one of them and bring him round our place for a Sunday dinner. Our mum would cook up a nice meal and, if our dad had any money to spare, he'd give him a couple of bob to help him on his way.

"When our mum was getting the lunch, we kids were all forced to drink a cup of cabbage water. Bloody awful stuff, but it was a way of giving us our vitamins and it didn't cost anything.

"Our dad used to come home from work, take his shoes and socks off and sit in his chair. Those grandfather chairs, every house in Great Britain had them. 'Here you are, Bronc,' he'd say. None of us were called by our real names. My brothers Dave and Geoffrey, they were Jerry and John, and my sister Jean was Sally. 'Here you are, Bronc, here's the razor blade.' And he'd give me a ha'penny if I cut his corns. He just sat there. He was so placid.

"I remember when we started playing cricket in the back yard. My brother John and me. Our dad was sat behind the window reading his paper, and I bowled this ball. It took off and went straight through the window; it showered him with glass. He never batted an eyelid, just called out to our mum, 'Hild'. She came rushing in the living room, wiped off all the glass, and he never even moved. Nothing upset him. Only drink. He'd fight the world if he'd been drinking, but he never laid hands on the family. 'If you don't answer back,' our dad said, 'you haven't got an argument.'

"I never ever lost my temper playing cricket. I used to think it was such a beautiful game, so superb, above people losing their tempers.

"Mary, give Stephen some more tomatoes. They're delicious, aren't they?

"I think my dad and his brothers must have gone to the Wagon Works ground, the day when Wally Hammond scored 300 in Tom Goddard's benefit match. 1936. I would have been six years old. They all talked about it. Perhaps they went up there after work like they used to in those days.

"Nottinghamshire were the visitors, and the belief in Gloucestershire was that Tom Goddard had a word with Wally. The game looked like it might be over in two days, and Tom Goddard was worried he might lose a day of his benefit takings. Hammond was supposed to have said, 'Don't worry, Tom, they won't even get me out.' It was a phenomenal innings. I don't think the rest of the team got much more than 150 between them.

"But years later I met Harold Larwood at Trent Bridge, and he told me a totally different story. Apparently, when Notts played Gloucester the previous year, they were playing on a green 'un, and Bill Voce took a fiendish delight in hitting Wally all over his body with the ball. 'I went up to Bill,' Harold told me, 'and I said, 'Look, Big 'Un, you might be enjoying yourself, but the bugger, he'll get his own back.' But Bill was so full of himself, he was going to knock his bloomin' head off, show him who was boss. So Hammond took his revenge on us in this game at the Wagon Works.' He went out purposefully to murder Bill Voce; he absolutely took him to pieces. 'Thank God I wasn't playing,' Harold said. It was nothing to do with Tom's benefit.

"I can still hear my dad and his brothers talking about it. One six he hit over the sight screen, over Tuffley Avenue, over the houses and into the hedges beyond that. And I listened. To me as a lad, I thought, 'Great stern stuff'. It never ever crossed my mind that I'd be a cricketer and play for Gloucestershire. Cricketers were heroes, untouchables."

"But how did you start playing, Bomber?"

"I was nine when the war started, and they brought in Double British Summer Time. It never seemed to get dark until nearly midnight in summer, and we used to play out in the streets from five or six and go on until eleven o'clock at night. And in summer it was always cricket. Just outside our house was a manhole cover. We used to stick bean sticks in it for our stumps, put down a coat or a jersey at the other end and play all evening. The Top of the Street versus the Bottom, that sort of thing. Sometimes it got up to about twenty a side. And there were no cars to worry about.

"Mr Hughes across the street made us a bat out of a piece of oak or elm. It was just like a proper bat, but it had a flat back. But we didn't mind, we didn't know any different. And we played with a tennis ball. It was like in the West Indies now. They never play with a hard ball, they're never frightened of being hit, so they get behind the ball. But it was a hard enough ball to break a few windows. 'Hey, watch it,' they'd shout, but we'd collect up half a crown and go down Raggy Small's on Gloucester Spa. Everybody went there for everything, from mangles to hammers and garden tools. And we'd buy these big pictures - like 'The Monarch of the Glen', that one of the stag. They had to be big pictures like that because Mr Hughes had to cut out the glass for the broken window. I reckon we must have spent most of our pocket money on those second-hand pictures. We had enough prints of shaggy Highland cattle to open an art gallery.

New Street, Gloucester

"Down the street in the spring, like so many streets in Gloucester, there'd be the elver-catchers. The tell-tale sign that they had elvers for sale was, they put a chair outside with a towel over it. They used to catch them from the Severn. A great Gloucestershire dish. 'Bronc,' my mum used to call to me. 'Bronc, go outside and see if the Barnes have got their towel out.' And if they had, 'Go and get two pounds. Here's a shilling.' These days the elvers go all over the world, Japan are the biggest gobblers of them, but they're so over-fished they cost 37 or 40 pounds a pound. They're the dearest fish in the world now, I suppose, but at one time they were the working man's meal in the Spring. I've known people who'd sit down and eat five or six pounds at a time. But all that's gone. Gloucester Rugby team used to be called the Elver Eaters. But I don't suppose there's more than one or two in a crowd of ten thousand now who've tasted them.

"To me, when I was young, it was a big street. These days it's all been done up, it looks quite nice, they're like town houses. But I look at it, and everyone's got a car, and I wonder how the hell we ever found room for our cricket. It looks so narrow. And the doors are all shut and the windows closed. In our day, on those double summer time evenings, people used to sit outside on the chairs, drinking cups of tea and nattering. The same conversation would start at one end of the street and go down to the other.

"You could walk a mile to Hempsted and you were in the country. I had an auntie in Hempsted. Auntie Lil, she was married to our dad's brother Harold. She was a real Romany. She used to make her own pegs and sell them, pick wild daffodils, catkins, bullrushes. The stuff we ate when we went there. 'God has provided everything for us,' she'd say. I reckon sometimes we were eating bloody cats. We wouldn't know any different. And gosh, could she talk. Tell you all about her childhood. We'd sit at the table, and she'd tell us how she used to take lurchers out to train with her father, to catch the rabbits and the hares, and how she'd pick snails and flog them. Snails, they were a nice delicacy in those days. But if she got too much to drink, she'd take on anyone. Bare-fist fights down the Colin Campbell. That was a notorious pub down by the docks. Our mum was absolutely disgusted.

"Then there was Auntie Violet in Churchdown. She was married to our dad's brother Bill, and he was a big man. Six foot two, six foot three. The family reckoned I followed Uncle Bill. I remember him as a fat man, very jolly. My father and his brothers, and my brothers too, they were thin, average people, but Uncle Bill was the biggie. Churchdown, that was a good five miles from our house. We used to go fishing, mushrooming, blackberrying. There were farms and fields whichever way you went. Then there was about four miles between that and Cheltenham before you saw anything else. I think there's about five hundred yards now.

"Our next-door neighbour-but one, Mr Best, he was the gateman on the locks. They used to bring all the timber up the canal for the Wagon Works and for Moreland's Matches. And the boats used to come up with all this raw chocolate on, it was going up to Cadbury's in Bournville, and they used to chuck Mr Best a great lump. I always think it was better than the proper chocolate. It was gorgeous.

"It's strange how things stick in your mind. I used to go with our mum into Eastgate Market in the city. She used to go to Rigby's, the big fresh fish merchant, and she'd wait until she caught Mr Rigby's eye. 'I want a piece of haddock, Mr Rigby,' she'd say, 'with a thumb and a finger mark on.' And he'd bring her a piece of beautiful haddock, turn it over, and there were these two marks on the back. It took me ages to find out - well, it took me ages to buck up courage to ask our mum. 'What's that thumb and finger mark all about then?' And she said, 'That's the way you tell real haddock. It's where Christ picked up the fish when he fed the multitude.'

"In the war our dad was classed as an essential worker. Whenever there'd been a heavy bombing raid on a big city, and skilled factory workers had been killed, our dad was called upon at the drop of a hat to go there to work. So he was away a lot during the war. But we had our dad's brother and sister staying with us, Uncle Dave and Auntie Joyce. And we only had two bedrooms. Our mum and Auntie Joyce shared the double bed, with our Jean in a single, and Uncle Dave and myself were in the other room.

"My mother was an extraordinary woman. She'd give away her last penny. During the war she got my sister and myself running errands for people - people who weren't quite well or had no money. And she had very little money herself.

"But New Street was marvellous. One old lady was so poor that she used to make herself a cup of tea on Monday morning and she'd keep straining the leaves till Tuesday night. And always on a Wednesday our mum used to make a big saucepan full of stew, with dumplings, and I used to take a helping down to her. And on a Sunday morning this old lady would take eight or ten of us for a walk, out to Hempsted, down to the Spa, along the course of the river and back along the railway line. And we used to pick up any pieces of coal we could find and put them in a large bag. She would sell her clothing coupons, even some of her food coupons. My mum used to tell my sister and me, 'However poor you are, there's always someone who is worse off than you.' And that old lady certainly was."

"But the cricket, Bomber. How did you move on from playing in the street?"

"Well, as we grew older and stronger, we hit the ball further so we went up the park."

I shut my lunch box.

"Would you like an apple?"

"No, it's all right, thank you, Bomber."

"Mary, give Stephen an apple."

I take a bite. "Did you play cricket at school?"

"Oh no. I went to St Paul's Elementary School, and I only remember the one game. We were challenging Calton Road Juniors, and our sports master, Mr Harris, was getting the side together. He took us out onto the tarmac playground and gave us all this trial. Every lad, whether he liked it or not, had to have a go. With the bat mainly. I went in, played my usual shot, and it went off the middle of the bat, over the top of the school, landed on Mrs Blackwell the caretaker's roof and bounced into the street. I had the strength, you see. He came up to me. I expected him to say 'Well hit', and he just smacked me round the earhole, called me a bloody fool. His little moustache quivered. "Don't just stand there, boy. Go and fetch it." Out I went through the wrought-iron gate. And I was never considered for the team. The actual game never took place, anyway, because a bomb fell in Gloucester and that was it.

"Then I went to Linden Road Secondary School, following in a long line of Wellses. Two or three generations had been there, but I found it rather dull. Many of the old teachers had retired and, with it being the war, the place was full of young women who'd only just left college. All they did was to read to us, read to us, read to us. Books like 'The Thirty-Nine Steps' and 'Treasure Island', hour-and-a-half or two-hour sessions. The school playing field had been turned into allotments, part of the Dig For Victory campaign, so we'd play stool ball in the playground and then in the winter hundred-a-side football.

"We had this woodwork master who tried to make us a bat. It looked lovely, but we could hardly lift it up. It must have weighed about six pounds. He was a Welshman, he had no idea. If we got hold of a bat, we'd drop it handle first onto the pavement, see how many times it bounced. Boom-boom, that's a two-springer. Boom-boom-boom, that's a three-springer. 'That's a better bat, that's a three-springer.' They were all things that kids did in those days. You lived in a world free of all this intense commercialism. You lived in your own little world, and you were satisfied with your lot.

"But stool ball was a good game for me. The striker used a little rounder's bat, and the pitcher threw the ball underarm at a square board fixed to a wooden post. Three lives, then you were out. I found I could deliver it about twice as fast as anybody else - and with great accuracy. I used to go boom, boom, boom, boom, boom, and our side would win. We never played any matches against other schools so I've no idea what standard I reached.

"The year I left, we found a kitbag full of cricket stuff, and we borrowed this. I had a word with Mr George, the headmaster. He'd taught my two brothers before me, and he allowed us to use it in the playground before school started. Then he let me take one of the bats home for the evening, and I'd take it up the park.

"In those days there was a park keeper who had a little sentry box, and he stood by the side of a huge first world war tank. From there he could look all the way round the park, make sure you didn't play on the side that was there for people picnicking. So we had to play on a rough piece of ground, and it was a dump. The ground was so uneven that, when the local fun fair set up, they couldn't get their carousels down level. It was during the fair that we moved on from the tennis ball. We used to hang around at the back of the coconut shy and pinch some of the balls. Then we'd take them home, and we'd put insulation tape all the way round them to make them the same size as cricket balls. Then we'd put tin tacs in them and cover them with french chalk from our puncture outfits, to take the tackiness away. But eventually the stickiness came through. I remember one time the boy batting came tearing down the pitch, and the ball just stuck in my fingers. All I had to do was lob it over his head and get him stumped.

"The coconut balls were very hard, though, and we didn't have pads. And, with the ground being so rough, my mates soon got fed up with my bowling fast. Every so often there was a regular little procession up to the hospital. So I took up bowling slow. And, because I used to bowl from five till eleven o'clock at night, I learnt the great art of standing still and bowling. It was much easier. If it was cold, I might take one or two steps. As Charlie Parker said to me years later, 'It's not what happens at this end that matters. It's what it does at the other end.' And I soon found that, if I bowled slow, the ball wouldn't fly off in all directions. I could pitch it on a length, beat the bat and hit the stumps.

"They had all these lovely horse chestnut trees in Gloucester Park, and I used to love to hit the ball over them. They were all cut down about three years ago.

They were rotting and dangerous. Now they've planted all little trees. I could hit the ball tremendous distances because I was so strong across the back and shoulders. But mostly I just wanted to bowl. Every evening and all weekend. I must have bowled fifty hours a week."

His friend Norman confirms Bomber's unquenchable enthusiasm. "A knock would come on my door. He'd be there on his bicycle, with his bat and ball. 'Come and have a bat, Norman,' he'd say. 'I want to do some bowling.' And it wasn't just summer. There'd be frost on the ground sometimes. The people in the park must have thought we were mad."

"My father was working in Brockworth by this time," Bomber says, "at the aircraft factory where they made the Gloucester Meteors. He'd walk up King Street into King's Square to catch his bus at six o'clock in the morning. Before the war the pubs used to open at that time so the workers could call in and have a rum or a whisky on the way to work. It helped to keep them warm. There was no heating in the factories, and most of the work was done outside. Anyway one morning he walked past John Bellows the printers, and there in the window were these two apprenticeships - one for a machine minder, one for a compositor. When he came home that evening, he said to me, 'You always want to have a trade behind you, Bronc. Have a word with Mr George tomorrow. Tell him that I want you to find out about these jobs.' And I did. I think that was on the Thursday, and on Monday I started. I missed out the last two months of school. I wasn't even fourteen.

"For a while that summer we gave up our cricket for baseball. The city had a sudden influx of American G.I.s, they came to train with the Gloucester Regiment, and we spotted them playing on the outfield of the Spa Cricket Ground. So for two or three weeks we joined in and fielded in their games. They were amazed that we fielded without mitts. Then they all went off. For the D-Day invasion, I suppose. And they presented us with their baseball and a pair of their mitts. So suddenly we had a pair of wicket-keeping gloves, and a baseball to bowl with. Now the baseball is similar in size and weight to a cricket ball, and it was the nearest thing to a cricket ball I'd ever had in my hands. So that's when I really got to bowling properly. I had something I could grip in my hand and control.

"After that we played all our cricket at the Spa. There was this groundsman. The Spa is a huge ground, with eighty or ninety yard boundaries, and he cut the whole of it with a hand mower. We used to watch out to see when he went home. As soon as he was gone, we were setting up stumps and enjoying the luxury of the smooth turf. And, as we grew older, we got that much more confident and actually pitched our stumps on the square. And we used to get these crowds, a hundred or two hundred people watching us play. With the war there was no sport on at all.

"That summer of 1944 I saw my first day of cricket. The R.A.F. against the West of England at the Wagon Works ground. It was my first sight of Hammond. The Wagon Works have got two pitches, side by side, and along this fence on the farther side there was this corrugated iron wall. It was the gents toilets. And my brother John and myself had gone in. Hammond was batting, and I'd just come out and there was a bang. He'd pulled this six. The ball went 130, 140 yards, and banged against the corrugated iron. I picked it up and threw it onto the second pitch, which was a good throw. And someone else picked it up and threw it back to the middle. It was an incredible distance.

"That summer I played my first organised game of cricket. For St James's Youth Club. It was a marvellous club, one of the first in Gloucester. It only closed down a year or so ago. Against the Civil Service Seconds, all a mixture of old and young 'uns. It was the first time I'd ever bowled with a proper cricket ball, and I took nine wickets.

"Where I was different from other bowlers was that I had tremendous strength across my chest and shoulders. I could pick up a hundredweight bag of spuds and just go whoop, bang on my shoulder, while the other lads would be struggling till they got it up there. That's why I could stand still and bowl. I had that strength across the chest.

"By the end of the war, the Etheridges had moved into New Street. Bobby was four years younger than me, and his parents were a bit strict on him not coming out. But who would have guessed that ten years later there'd be two New Street boys in the Gloucestershire team?"

"So there I was. Out of all that - listening to my dad and his brothers in front of the fire, the broken windows in the street, the stool ball in the playground, the coconut balls in the park - one day I found I could play cricket. It's amazing really when you think about it. But it still never ever occurred to me that I would play for Gloucestershire."

The umpires are replacing the bails, the fielders finding their positions, and our attention turns once more to today's game. Here in 1999 the outfield reveals a handful of children with bats, returning with their fathers to their seats, no streets for them to learn their cricket. But in 1957 the whole outfield is criss-cross with lunch-time cricket matches.

"Did your parents ever watch you playing, Bomber?"

"My dad did once. I was playing for the Harlequins against Bristol Tramways, and he walked over from the pub with three of his brothers. I think I got eight wickets that day. 'Well done, Bronc,' he said, 'but don't let it go to your head.'"

"And your mum? She was alive when you were playing county cricket, wasn't she?"

"She came down to Stroud once with my brother. She arrived just as I was leading off the team. But I don't think she ever saw me bowl. She said she didn't have the time. She'd rather go out and have a natter with her friends in the street."

JOURNEYMEN AT WORK

The afternoon of the first day

The Gloucestershire team return to the field, led by their regular captain, George Emmett. Born in India, the son of a soldier, he has spent the six years of the war in the desert and in Italy, and he brings a military discipline to his captaincy. He is 44 now, among county cricket's oldest players, and he is one of the first professionals to be appointed a captain.

G. M. EMMETT

A short man. An apprentice upholsterer who was plucked from club cricket in Torquay. An attacking batsman who spent his early years under the half-disapproving eye of Wally Hammond. A county stalwart who was picked once for England in 1948, made ten and nought against the pace of Lindwall and was never considered again. A professional captain in an age when the idea is still an anathema to many counties.

"He was like a lot of short people in authority," Bomber says. "He had to make his little frame look important. He had this strutting walk. When Peter Rochford was playing, he used to walk along behind him, imitating him. He had all the mannerisms. He used to call him Captain Bligh."

Captain Bligh. The dormobile that carries the team kit is nicknamed The Bounty. But Peter Rochford's mutiny is over now; he has played his last game for Gloucestershire.

"Or people called Emmett SM. Sergeant-Major."

His daughter Gill smiles. "He was promoted to Sergeant-Major in the War, but he relinquished it. Said he'd rather be one of the boys."

"I never knew he'd been an upholsterer," Bomber says. "Now you mention it, though, he was always telling people to get stuffed."

"He had a glare that would melt icicles," Gill says, "and there was always me on the end of it."

"When we were ready to go out," Bomber says, "we had to stand up and show him our boots, to see if we had all the studs in. And we never went out in flannels with stains on. Then in the field you had to look at him after every ball to see if he was wanting to move you. And you had to stay where you were put. 'When I put you in a position,' he'd say, 'stay in that position. Make a mark.' In the end he got complaints from Bernie Bloodworth, the groundsman. There were marks all over the square."

"He had such attention to detail," Tony Brown says. "People talk about captaincy. It's about controlling the game when you're in the field. He never seemed to miss anything. He was always moving you, and always he'd give you a reason. And it never slowed the game down like it does these days. Even David Smith and I used to bowl twenty overs an hour with the new ball."

"You didn't do anything to bring the game into disrepute," Bomber says. "If you were out, you walked, no matter what. And if somebody took a great catch, you didn't dare to applaud. 'He's paid to do that,' he'd say. 'There's enough exhibitionism in cricket without your adding to it.'"

It is not just on the pitch, either. "When I went to Cheltenham," Gill remembers, "I wasn't allowed to go round the other side of the ground and run around with the hoi polloi. I'd got to remember who I was and behave myself."

It is all too much for Peter Rochford, but Bomber looks back with admiration.

"Old Emmett was easily the best captain we had. Everyone will tell you that. He read the game so well, and he played to win. He was like a hunter, going for the kill. He always attacked. And he had such a tremendous love for the game. It rubbed off on every one."

Here at Cheltenham in 1957 *'the wind and sun had done its work well during the luncheon adjournment. One over from Smith showed that the wicket had lost its fire for the fast bowler. It was up to Wells and Cook to try to finish the job.'*

"All through my career," Bomber says, "I could smell if the wicket was going to turn. It was lovely when you were bowling and you got that smell."

Wells and Cook. The journeymen of county cricket. George Emmett may once have been an apprentice upholsterer, but Bomber and Sam still ply their trades. In winter Bomber is a printer in the city of Gloucester, Sam a plumber in the small town of Tetbury. In summer they are slow bowlers both. Sam the placid craftsman, a thin man, his receding hair combed flat on his scalp, rolling - not spinning - the ball out of his left hand. Bomber the excitable joker, a large man with hair that sits up in spikes, mixing his unorthodox off-spin with all sorts: away swingers, leg-breaks, quicker balls, flighted ones. "Sam was fantastic," he says. "He'd just bowl away, every ball on the spot, never experiment. But me, it used to bore me silly to bowl two balls the same."

Famous Cricketers
No. 16   Set of 40

B. D. WELLS
(Gloucestershire)
Born Gloucestershire 1930. Made his debut in 1951, and was awarded his County cap in 1954. Developed rapidly as an off-break bowler, and in 1953 took 8 Somerset wickets for 31 runs at Taunton. A bowler with a great future, and a hard-hitting batsman.
Issued by
CLEVEDON
CONFECTIONERY
(Blackpool) LTD.
Blackpool - England.

'In Wells's next over Illingworth hit three loose balls for four to reach his fifty.'

Cook and Wells. Cricket's great reputations are made in the Test match arena and, if you ask people to name the great Gloucestershire bowlers of the second half of the twentieth century, they will start with Mike Procter and Courtney Walsh, then they will turn to the off-spinners, Allen and Mortimore, and maybe they will add as an afterthought 'dear old Sam Cook', as if their affection exceeds his achievement.

Perhaps we should look at the facts and figures. Let's take all the Gloucestershire matches of the last fifty years of the century and see which bowlers have the best averages:

Gloucestershire 1950-1999

		Wickets	Average
1	Mike Procter	833	19.56
2	Courtney Walsh	869	20.01
3	Sam Cook *	1283	20.03
4	Bomber Wells	544	21.18
5	David Allen	882	22.13
6	Tom Goddard *	219	22.17
7	John Mortimore	1696	22.69
8	David Smith	1159	23.68

* not their full career figures

"People who read cricket books," Bomber says, "don't want to read all these bloody statistics. They like stories."

"But everybody on that list, Bomber, except for you, played Test cricket. Did you ever think you'd get selected?"

"Oh, no. There were so many good off-spinners in those days: Jim Laker, Roy Tattersall, Robin Marlar."

"But take the summer of 1954. They picked Jim McConnon of Glamorgan ahead of all of them. Would it have been so far-fetched for them to pick you?"

"I don't know. I used to look at bowlers, and I'd say to myself, 'He's a good bowler.' I never used to think, 'Well, I'm as good as him' or 'I'm better than him.' I just enjoyed playing with them, laughing and joking. Maybe if I hadn't had such a come-day, go-day attitude, the powers-that-be might have appreciated me more."

Gloucestershire have off-spinners a-plenty in the 1950s, and David Allen and John Mortimore will both progress into Test cricket. "But in some ways," Brian Close says, "Bomber was the one you feared most because of his unusualness." Ken Biddulph agrees: "Down at Somerset we all thought he was the best of the three." He certainly would not have suffered from nerves if he had had to step out in a Test match at Lord's, but in 1954 maybe his rolling gait and his rough-and-ready ways would not have been acceptable.

The previous August at Lord's Bomber had played for the Combined Services against the Public Schools. "They had this boy Robins bowling to Ingleby-Mackenzie. He was supposed to be a leg-break bowler, but he completely lost control, started bowling little seamers, right up Ingleby's street. I was on the balcony, and I turned to this chap next to me. 'I thought this idiot bowled leg-breaks.' And he stood up and stared at me. 'I never comment on my son's cricket,' he said, and off he went." R.W.V. Robins, Middlesex Secretary and Test selector. "Thirty years later I met his wife. 'He never did forgive you,' she said."

Here at Cheltenham Bomber is happy to be playing for Gloucestershire.

'Sutcliffe moved out to hit Wells but failed to connect properly and was caught at mid-on.'

Sutcliffe, caught Smith, bowled Wells, 18   Yorkshire, 115 for six

Johnny Wardle steps out to bat. "He only had the one way to play," Bomber says, and George Emmett makes his adjustments in anticipation. *'The field spread wider for Wardle who responded by clouting Cook twice to leg.'* But Sam is no fool, and Wardle's life proves *'a short and merry one'* when *'Graveney held a catch at cover to give Cook his first wicket in the match.'*

Wardle, caught Graveney, bowled Cook, 5   Yorkshire, 120 for seven

Sam Cook did play Test cricket. But, like George Emmett his captain, like Charlie Parker his left-arm predecessor, like Mike Smith, Gloucestershire's left-arm seamer in the 1990s, it was just the once. At Trent Bridge in 1947.

Perhaps he was lucky to play at all. In 1946, Sam's first summer, Yorkshire complained that the Bristol pitch was dead, and they put Colonel Henson in touch with the Bingley Research Centre. The following May they arrived to find a square filled with sand and were bowled out for 128, Cook nine for 42. By a happy turn of fortune, England's captain Norman Yardley was among his victims and that weekend the team for the first Test was selected.

But then again, perhaps he was unlucky to play on a flat batting paradise at Trent Bridge. South Africa, 533 and 166 for one. Tom Goddard took him aside before he set off: "Sam, if you've got any sense, you want to call off sick while you have time." Perhaps he used up his luck the previous summer when he was selected for a Test trial at Canterbury on a wicket that was made for him. But then that was in the week he had been given off to get married, and the Canterbury trip became his honeymoon. "If I'd bowled anything like I could," he wrote in his memoir, "I must have stood a great chance of going to Australia but alas it was one of those days. I sat down at lunch right opposite Hammond who just looked at me and said, 'What's the matter, Cooky, spending too many nights in the saddle?'"

Perhaps this Cotswold plumber was going to take longer than one Test to feel at ease with Hutton and Bedser, Compton and Edrich. "I think, if I'd been playing with the Gloucester lads," he said years later, "I'd have felt really at home."

It is ten years ago now. The debate has moved on to the merits of Wardle and Lock, and Sam is content to be a county cricketer. He bowls here at Cheltenham, hoping the sun will last and that he will have his bungalow over the hill. The entertainment of Wardle the batsman is over, but more might be in store with the arrival of Fred Trueman.

Fred is averaging nearly 18 this summer, a big hitter like Bomber but, he will tell you, 'a proper batsman' as well. He walks to the wicket with purpose. What a pity his partner today does not share his faith in his ability.

Sam Cook

49

'The sight of Trueman approaching seemed to convince Illingworth that he must adopt desperate measures. He hit Wells for two fours before attacking the wrong ball from Cook, spooning it to Emmett in the covers.'

Illingworth, caught Emmett, bowled Cook, 70   **Yorkshire, 129 for eight**

Sam Cook. What did Wally Hammond see in the young man from Tetbury when he came down to Bristol for that 1946 trial? "He saw a natural slow left-arm bowler," John Arlott says on a BBC tribute to Sam. "Not a prodigious spinner, no great flight, no great subtlety but after an absolute accuracy. And Sam could turn it on a responsive wicket, enough to beat the bat and that was enough for most people." On grainy, old film Sam runs in to bowl at the Wagon Works, Arthur Milton sprints from slip to take a catch, and Bomber watches from his arm chair. "What a beautiful follow through," he says. "You don't see people bowling with an action like that now, do you?"

The television camera settles on the heavy, sad-eyed face of John Arlott. "I think the most tragic piece of change that cricket has undergone is the debasing of the slow bowler and everything that goes with it. Sam would have rubbed his hands at the sight of rain and gone on and bowled on a sticky and made it go."

Bomber smiles. "Old Charlie Parker used to say, 'Rain never comes to help the batsman.'" Then he too catches Arlott's mood. "If I were fit now," he says, looking down at his sticks, "I reckon in a short time I could turn twenty of the country's medium pacers into off-spinners or slow left-armers."

"Bomber was looking after one of the teams at the King's School in Gloucester," a schoolmaster once told me. "I took a side to play there, and he met me with a huge grin. 'We're going to have a really good game today,' he said. 'I've got a bowling attack of four off-spinners.'"

Yorkshire are eight wickets down, and Bomber bowls to Fred Trueman.

"I don't know why people ever worried about Fred's batting," Bomber says. "He was the easiest person in the world to kid out. I played against him at Lord's for the Army against the R.A.F. The summer he made his Test debut, took all those Indian wickets. There was a big crowd, and they all cheered him in. I warned him I was going to bowl him a bouncer. 'I'll bloody bouncer you,' he said. And I bowled this ball so slow, he was on his third wrap-around when it hit his stumps."

It is no better here at Cheltenham.

Trueman, bowled Wells, 0   **Yorkshire, 129 for nine**

Then Sam bowls to Jimmy Binks, and David Smith jumps *'high at mid-on to take a truly amazing, one-handed catch.'* In twenty minutes Yorkshire have lost their last five wickets for 18 runs, all to Cook and Wells.

Binks, caught Smith, bowled Cook, 2   **Yorkshire, 133 all out**

In a total of 133, Ray Illingworth has made 70, and he was dropped before he scored.

YORKSHIRE

W.B. Stott	b Smith	0
W. Watson	c Milton b Smith	3
D.E.V. Padgett	c Etheridge b Brown	18
D.B. Close	c Mortimore b Brown	7
J.V. Wilson	c Milton b Smith	8
R. Illingworth	c Emmett b Cook	70
*W.H.H. Sutcliffe	c Smith b Wells	18
J.H. Wardle	c Graveney b Cook	5
F.S. Trueman	b Wells	0
+J.G. Binks	c Smith b Cook	2
D. Pickles	not out	2
Extras		0
		133

1-1, 2-4, 3-15, 4-28, 5-38, 6-115, 7-120, 8-129, 9-129, 10-133

Smith	14	4	27	3
Brown	14	7	24	2
Cook	14.4	3	36	3
Mortimore	4	0	11	0
Wells	10	2	35	2

Within five minutes the Yorkshire team is taking the field, led by Billy Sutcliffe, and Fred Trueman is marking out his long run. 'A visiting Test team from a distant Northern kingdom,' John Light calls them. Surrey may have won their sixth successive championship yesterday, but Yorkshire are still the team everybody wants to beat. "They were very proud of their side," Bomber tells. "Very, very proud. If you did beat them, it was the season's greatest feat. More even than beating Surrey."

"Everyone played just that little bit harder against Yorkshire," Brian Close says. "Every match was a needle match. And no Yorkshireman ever wanted it any other way."

Yorkshire is only for the Yorkshire-born, but this is no problem in the 1950s. Indeed there is a strong Yorkshire-born team to be found among the players of the other sixteen counties: Brookes, Barker, Hamer, Lee, van Geloven, Barrick, Booth, Bennett, Laker, Shackleton and Greensmith. And this week the news has broken that Willie Watson is moving to Leicestershire to join them. Why, with all these resources at their disposal, have Yorkshire achieved so little since the war?

Yorkshire, 1947-58. Hutton, Wardle, Lowson, Appleyard, Watson, Trueman, Close. They manage just one shared championship.

Yorkshire, 1959. Trueman and Close survive, Illingworth has emerged, and they are joined by Taylor, Stott, Padgett and Don Wilson. They win seven titles in ten years.

"The previous side was star-studded," Ken Taylor says. "Individually they were much better than we were, but they played for themselves. They were all batting for their averages or wanting to be bowling at nine, ten, jack. In the '60s we played for each other."

So what was it like playing against Yorkshire in the 1950s?

"They argued like hell amongst each other," Tom Graveney recalls, "but, if you dared to interfere, it was none of your business."

Or, as Leicestershire's Maurice Hallam once said to me, "They were always arguing but, when you tried to argue against them, you came up against a brick wall. They were one clan, Yorkshire for Yorkshiremen."

Most of this Gloucester side are Gloucestershire men, too. Eight of them are county born and bred, Tom Graveney moved here at the age of ten, and George Emmett came up from Torquay 21 years ago. Only Martin Young is a real outsider. "He was a public school boy," Bomber says. "His father was a director of the Midland Bank. He had this lah-di-dah voice. We were just ordinary chaps, and he was sat there, talking away as if he was a member of the Royalty. But he was a lovely chap. He used to go everywhere with Sam Cook."

"He'd been in the Navy," Tom Graveney remembers. "We used to call him The Commodore."

Martin Young throws in his lot with these West Countrymen. He hits 1000 runs in a season thirteen times, but he is never once invited to play for the M.C.C.

"It was so nice playing for your own county," Bomber says, and in 1957 it does not need homecoming exiles to make a crowd to watch them.

Martin Young walks to the wicket with George Emmett. The public school boy turned professional and the Sergeant-Major turned captain. In his one Test match Emmett was found wanting by the pace of Lindwall, but he still relishes the challenge of taking on the quick bowlers. Today Fred Trueman.

By contrast, Martin Young is a little apprehensive against the very quickest. As on that morning last summer at The Oval. "Peter Loader was like a stick of rhubarb," Tom Graveney says, "and he had this nasty aggressive streak. We were four for two overnight, we'd been out for a few beers, and Youngy was feeling a bit delicate. 'Morning, Peter,' he said, when we passed Loader. 'How's the wife?' 'You get down the other bloody end, and I'll show you how the bloody wife is.' Youngy went white. After three overs he walked down to me: 'Tom, I'm not feeling very well. Will you look after Loader?'" A lovely story, and Wisden provides the ending: *'Young, caught Swetman, bowled Loader, 133.'*

For years Yorkshire have been looking for a new ball partner for Fred Trueman, and in the last month they think they have finally discovered the answer: David Pickles. "He was terrifyingly fast," Brian Close says. "When he came in late that season he rolled over one side after another. But that winter the coaches got hold of him."

"He was a tall lad with a high action," Bryan Stott recalls, "and he had such speed. We were playing Notts at Trent Bridge, and he and Fred were bowling in partnership. He was so fast that Gamini Goonesena was trying to stay at Fred's end. And Fred wasn't one to be outdone so he was bowling at top speed. I was fielding at short leg, and Freddie Stocks was so nervous he couldn't stop talking."

But Bill Bowes is the Yorkshire coach, and in the winter he tries to remodel David's action on his own. "Bill got him crossing his legs before the delivery stride, which Bill himself used to do, and he couldn't bowl. He used to trip up, he bowled no balls and wides. If he'd been left alone, he'd have been wonderful. He was such a natural bowler."

Today at Cheltenham, though, the pitch is not suited to fast bowling. *'Fears that Trueman and Pickles might find the wicket to their liking were quickly stilled by Emmett and Young.'*

It is 41 for no wicket and the spinners are on before the first breakthrough. Martin Young edges Wardle into the slips, and Ron Nicholls soon follows.

Young, caught Trueman, bowled Wardle, 13
Nicholls, caught Wilson, bowled Illingworth, 1   Gloucestershire, 52 for two

George Emmett is *'batting delightfully'*, and he is joined at the wicket by Tom Graveney, back in favour as an England batsman and finally fulfilling his potential: 258 at Trent Bridge last month, 164 next week at The Oval. It is hard to understand how after such scores he continues not to command a regular place.

"I scored three consecutive Test hundreds at Trent Bridge and two in a row at The Oval," Tom says, "but they took me nine years." After 1957, he will score hundreds in '62 and '66 at Trent Bridge and a hundred at The Oval in '66. And he will miss all the matches in between.

"I don't think he was ever secure," Bomber says. "He was such a magnificent player, yet he'd read the paper and worry about all these other batsmen making runs. Absolutely amazing. I mean, Gary Sobers never read the paper. And I don't think Denis Compton did."

"I never thought I was a very good player until later on," Tom says. "I wouldn't say I worried. I just played. But I walked in the dressing room with Len Hutton and Denis Compton, Bedser and Evans …"

The sentence trails away, but it leaves me wondering. Sam Cook, one Test: "I think, if I'd been playing with the Gloucester lads, I'd have felt really at home."

Arthur Milton, a century on his debut, but only five more Tests: "It wasn't my scene," he told me. "I liked to play with the lads I knew." Even perhaps George Emmett: "the family always resented that he only played that once," Gill says, "especially when you see some of the people now, how dismal they are and how they still get selected."

It is tea at Cheltenham and, with Emmett and Graveney to come back out, there is every prospect of some entertainment in the evening.

Emmett, not out, 25
Graveney, not out, 2   **Gloucestershire, 55 for two**

A CAREER IN STORIES

Tea on the first day

The crowd claps George Emmett as he returns to the pavilion, and all round the ground hands reach into picnic baskets.

"Would you like a slice of our fruit cake?"

"Not for the moment, thank you, Bomber."

What about the cricketers? Do they eat when they are playing?

"If my father was batting," Gill Emmett tells, "he'd just have a cup of tea and a cigarette."

"I never used to bother," Sam Cook says on an old television interview. "'You can't bowl on food,' Tom Goddard told me. 'Just have a pint of beer and sweat that out.'"

"I used to sit next to Sam," Bomber says, "so I could have the extra cake, the extra sandwiches. It's always been the same. I think I've got a fatal attraction. Eating was a second pastime to me. It still is.

"Mary, pass Stephen a slice of fruit cake."

I remember the first time I met Bomber. I was researching my first book. *'Runs in the Memory: County Cricket in the 1950s'*, and his name had cropped up in most of my interviews. "He must have been the funniest person ever to play professional cricket," Derbyshire's David Green told me.

I arrived at ten o'clock with my pocket tape recorder and three 90-minute cassettes. "I'll only take a couple of hours," I had said on the phone but sometimes, if the memories flowed, I could get through two 90-minute tapes. The third was like the spare batteries, 'just in case'.

"Do you want stories?" he asked as Mary supplied the tea and biscuits. He sat in his armchair, looking across the field to the ever-humming Gloucester ring road, and I sat on the sofa at his side. "Stories it is, then," and he was away. Lunch came and went, and at three o'clock the third of my cassettes clicked to a halt. "I was at mid-wicket, this old dear said to me, 'Do you want a cuppa?', and suddenly this ball was coming towards me. So I put the cup in my left hand and ..." Furiously I scribbled.

"I have to be in Stroud at four," I said, but we carried on. "I think they tried every bowler on the ground before they tried me. Sir Derrick even bowled himself."

At half past four I stood up. Mary had taken the old dog for three walks, the sun was dropping towards the horizon, and the rush hour traffic was building up on the ring road. "I really must go, Bomber," I said, and he looked crestfallen. "But I haven't finished the story of my debut yet."

Tea time at Cheltenham. It is a chance to ask him how his story-telling began.

"Colonel Henson called me into his office at the end of my first full season. 'Bryan,' he said, 'You've got to go out and make yourself known to the members. Because they pay your wages. Never ignore them.' He gave me this list of speaking engagements for the winter. It was like a fixture card.

"The first one was in Cheltenham. I must have been terrible. I mean, I'd hardly had any education. I read from all these bits of paper, but they were very patient. This old man came up afterwards. 'Well done,' he said, 'but you don't want to worry about the notes. Talk from the brain. And keep your head up, look to the back, then every one will think you're talking to them.'

"In time I developed this knack. I found I could get hold of an incident, which was really nothing, and turn it into a marvellous story. That's all that people who go to cricket dinners want to hear. And they want to know what makes players click. They don't want all these bloody statistics.

"Later, when I was in Nottingham, I used to go all over the country. My neighbour said, 'You'll go anywhere for a free meal, Bomber.' Speaking's easy, as long as you don't try to be clever."

"So what are your favourite stories, Bomber?"

"Back in the '40s I played for a couple of years for the Gloucester Nondescripts. The Nondies. We only played away matches. Went out by charabanc. Had a sing-song. 'Ghost Riders In The Sky', 'She Wore Red Feathers'. All the families used to come. Anyway, we played at Witney one day, and they had this chap Len Hemming who played for Oxfordshire. Wonderful player. Well, I came off my one pace run, and I bowled him. And as he was going off, Bill Hook said to our skipper Jack Stevens, 'I don't think he was looking when Bomber bowled him. I'll get him to come back.' We played all away matches, you see, and we didn't like to offend anyone. So he came back rather sheepishly, and I bowled him next ball as well. And everyone started laughing. Well, Bill turned to Jack Stevens again. But before he could say a word, Len Hemming swung round. 'If you think I'm staying here for him to get his bloody hat-trick, you've got another think coming.' And off he went."

"The Nondescripts had a very useful side," Len Hemming tells me. "We had some wonderful games." And this story? "I've no recollection of it at all," he says, "but I'm all in favour of it."

"I was courting and I was out in the park in Gloucester," Bomber tells. "It was a lovely evening, about half past nine or ten. We were eating fish and chips, and this huge chap came across. Old Tom Goddard, his picture was in the paper every other day. 'Are you Bomber Wells? … Get down to Bristol tomorrow. You're playing against Sussex.'"

Bomber's debut for Gloucestershire. Ten days previously he made a single second eleven appearance - six for 51 in each innings - and now he was replacing the legendary Goddard. "Ron Nicholls and David Allen were coached along in the seconds," Gill Emmett remembers. "I knew their names before they started playing for the first team. Whereas Bomber just appeared."

"I went down on the bus. I had my kit in a large brown paper carrier. There must have been twenty Gloucester supporters, and we talked of nothing else but the game. But I never let on that I was playing."

"He was just a boy from the sticks," Arthur Milton recalls. "He strolled in, changed, came out. Nothing phased him. And he kept getting people out."

"As far as I was concerned, it was like playing for any other side I'd played for. I just wanted to go out and have a bowl.

"I was put in the gully, and there wasn't a third man. Well, the ball went past me, and I thought, 'That's gone, no need to run for that.' Jack Crapp was in the slips. 'If I were you, son,' he said, 'I'd go after that.' I think they ran five. ... I think they tried every bowler on the ground before they tried me. Sir Derrick even bowled himself."

Sir Derrick Bailey is Gloucestershire's amateur captain, the son of Abe Bailey who sold his South African diamond mines for a fortune. "Cooky said he owned half Hereford. He used to come to matches in this Lagonda with straw in his hair and boots with cow muck on. They can, people like that, can't they?"

It was 120 for one when Sir Derrick finally turned to Bomber and, according to the Gloucester Citizen, *'he immediately showed he could spin and twice went past the left-handed Smith's bat with his off-breaks.'* With Bomber's jaunty two or three pace run, there is even a story that Sir Derrick at mid-off only saw three balls of the over. "They say he turned round and walked back to his mark after the first ball," Tony Brown says, "and by the time he turned round Bomber was bowling the third one." *'Then he bowled a leg-break which turned so much that Smith almost played on.'*

"The Sussex batsmen had never seen anything like it," Tom Graveney tells. "I remember Jim Langridge batting. Very dour. Suddenly Bomber slipped the old back-spinner in, and it only just missed the leg stump. George Cox at the non-striker's end was falling about with laughter."

"They didn't have a clue," Bomber says. His first victim was David Sheppard, lbw playing back. "Bomber was so strong," Arthur Milton explains. "The ball used to pitch that much further up to you than what you thought. People were playing back to half-volleys." By the close of the innings, he had bowled 25 overs and taken six for 47. Then in the second innings he sent down another 36 overs. "I was his first county wicket," David Sheppard recalls, and he tells another story. "He went back into the dressing room after the match. 'Well,' he said. 'I can see, if I'm going to play for this side, I'm going to have to do a lot of bowling. I shall have to cut my run down.'"

Gill Emmett compares him with Sam Cook. "Sam was lovely to watch. I used to think he was like Dad batting. He was so graceful. But Bomber just shuffled up and chucked his arm over."

"I could bowl standing still. If you're a natural, everything comes easy. You can do what you like and get away with murder. If you're coached, unless you stay in that groove, you're struggling, aren't you?"

"Bomber was a very good bowler indeed," Sam Cook wrote in his memoir, "but boy was it hard work bowling at the other end. I always thought I was bowling without a break. And when asked what end he wanted, it was always with the wind as he said the wind blowing in his face made his eyes run."

"At Worcester I bowled this over to Roly Jenkins," Bomber tells. "We started as the cathedral clock was beginning to chime twelve. It was all arranged. I bowled it, and Jenks pushed every one down the wicket. I finished it before the chimes were done, and Sir Derrick came across. 'What do you think you're doing?' 'Not much,' I said. 'You're making the game look ridiculous.'"

"Sir Derrick told him to start his run further back," Tom Graveney tells. "So he sent him back about eight yards, and Bomber just took his two or three paces and let it go from where he was. And he pitched it right on a length."

"Sir Derrick went berserk," Bomber continues. "He dropped me for two matches, but it was worth it."

After that there were two years of National Service. In Chilwell near Nottingham with the Royal Army Ordnance Corps. "Rob All Our Comrades, they nicknamed us. It was the biggest fiddle. You used to see squaddies walking round with sheets of paper in their hands. 'He's busy,' people would think.

"The General was a great Gloucestershire man, and he was always letting me off to play for the county. Every time I had a weekend's leave I used to go up and see him, and he'd get his batman to fill a bag up with bacon and eggs, cheese and all sorts. 'Take that home to your mother,' he would say.

"During the second winter my mum got taken into hospital to have an operation on a goitre, and I was excused for three or four months. When I got back to camp, there was these East Coast floods. They made a terrible mess of places like Cleethorpes, took great chunks out of the sea wall. 'You,' this sergeant said, 'down to Cleethorpes.' They had a special Land Rover all fixed up, drove me down, and when I got there it was dark. I was just being shown my billet when a big 'Hooray' went up. The alert was over after a fortnight of hard slog. Then Prince Philip announced on the radio that all personnel involved were to have a week's leave, all expenses paid. So I went back to Chilwell and joined the queue. It was like a holiday camp, really."

A county cap in 1954, 122 and 123 wickets in the next two summers. But 1957 started less successfully. "We went down to Hove, and it had rained so much the pitch was like a quagmire. Cooky and I were going into Brighton for the day. 'Where are you two going?' Emmett said. 'We're playing.' He never gave up. He'd agreed with Marlar the Sussex skipper that they'd mark a pitch right on the edge of the square. The boundary couldn't have been more than thirty yards on the pavilion side."

On the last afternoon Sussex were set 267 in just over three hours, and the final session of play was mayhem. *'Almost before the rattle of tea cups had died away, Smith let loose a flush of fours and sixes mostly directed at the short leg-side boundary, scoring 27 in two overs off the luckless Wells.'* Then two overs of Derek Hawkins' occasional off-breaks produced another 33, and *'one unlucky spectator in the pavilion was struck by a hit for six and taken to hospital with a suspected fracture of the jaw.'*

"You've never seen such an exodus from the pavilion," Bomber tells. "They were trying to put this chap onto a stretcher, and every other ball was flying towards them. 'Well tried, Derek,' Emmett said. 'Take a rest.' And he signalled me back. A chap ran out on the field, pointing at me with this little umbrella. 'Take him off,' he said. 'I insist. He'll get some one killed.'"

In 1959 Bomber lost his place to David Allen, and by the following summer he was a Notts player, bowling on Trent Bridge's glorious batting tracks. Sam Cook made his one Test appearance there, nought for 127 in 30 overs: "What do you want to go up there for, Bomb? You'll end up being cannon fodder." But Tony Brown saw it differently - "The great thing about Bomber was that he was such a good bowler on good pitches." - and his first summer there yielded 120 wickets.

Notts were a struggling side in the early '60s, and Bomber's first 15 matches brought just one victory - against Somerset at Bath. "It was sweltering. We had Roger Vowles making up numbers for us. He was secretary of our Supporters' Club, and he turned red as a turkey cock in the heat. Bill Alley pushed this ball past him. He ran down towards the boundary, and this great Alsatian dog appeared. Every time he went to pick up the ball, it bared its teeth and snarled. In the end they signalled four and got another ball. And after that the crowd really took to Roger. Whenever the ball came near him, they all started barking.

"On the last afternoon we were in a run chase, and Reg Simpson told us to take our chairs and our kit down to the boundary edge to save time. Cyril Poole was batting magnificently, and Roger was next man in. He sat there working through this packet of cigarettes, and suddenly Pooly hit this ball up in the air. It looked like it was going straight down Peter Wight's throat. 'Go on, get out there,' I said. 'Don't waste time.' He jumped up like a startled hare and belted off for the middle. What a sight it was! A fag in his hand, no sign of a bat. The ball sailed away for six, and he had to walk all the way back off. Talk about a turkey cock. He was every shade of red."

Five years later Bomber's first-class career was over. He took four Northants wickets at Wellingborough, then he was dropped for the last time. "Some statistician worked out that I'd taken 999 wickets so they offered me the game against Gloucester at Bristol. They said, 'Somebody down there will give you their wicket.' But I said, 'No. Plenty of people have got a thousand wickets. I bet no one's got 999.'"

Bomber is not one to dwell on statistics - not unless they make a good story. He sighs with regret. "Three months later they found I'd only got 998."

The last wicket may have been taken, but the stories go on. Up and down the country, at Cricket Society meetings and charity lunches he has told them. "I want you, Bryan, to make yourself known to the members," Colonel Henson said. "Never ignore them." And he never has.

"He stayed at my house after the meeting," one Cricket Society member told me. "He sat down in the front room, and he was still going strong at two in the morning."

"I've met Bomber Wells," somebody else told me. "Who hasn't?"

He sits in his wheelchair by the scorebox, and he will happily natter with anyone who wants to sit down beside him, all in his broad Gloucester accent.

"When I worked for Boots in Nottingham, this woman used to ring me up at least twice a week. 'Bomber, do me a favour,' she'd say. 'Say pork sausages.' And I'd say 'pork sausages'. 'That's lovely,' she said. 'I'm having some for tea, and you've made them all the better for saying it.'"

But not everybody stays true to their own voice.

"I spoke at a dinner at the Hilton for John Emburey," Bomber tells. "I was on my way downstairs to the toilet, and I went through this room where a smart-looking chap was sitting on his own at a bar. 'A lovely day, isn't it?' he said in a really posh, educated voice. I looked at him, and I said, 'What are you talking like that for? You're Peter Rochford.' 'Who are you then? … Oh Bomber.' And he started talking properly. He'd come up from Stroud to write a report for the Telegraph on Jim Laker's funeral."

Caught Rochford, bowled Wells. Back in 1956, when Jim Laker was the hero of all England, they combined to capture many a wicket. But by the end of 1957 their paths had parted. Bomber looks back on the fun of it all, enough stories to fill a lifetime of speeches, but Peter?

"The last time I saw him was at the Wagon Works. He'd had an operation for cancer, and he called me back. 'I had this nightmare beforehand,' he said. 'I dreamt the surgeon was Captain Bligh.'"

"Peter Rochford was a fool to himself," Tony Brown says. "He had great talent. He could have been a top quality cricketer."

And Bomber, was he a fool? He played the fool certainly.

"Essex had this young amateur batting for them one time," Bomber says, "and he kept stepping away when I was trying to bowl. And I've no idea why I did it, maybe I wanted to teach him a lesson, but I ran all the way round the square, past mid-on, square leg, behind the keeper, back to mid-off, and I shouted out, 'Are you ready now?' And I bowled him first ball."

"We were out looking at the wicket at Rushden," Arthur Milton recalls, "and this music comes over the public address. He's only got the secretary to put his record on."

"Ah, yes," Bomber smiles. "That was Les Paul and Mary Ford. He was a superb guitar player, wasn't he? The first one who electrified them."

'Somewhere there's music - how faint the tune.
Somewhere there's heaven - how high the moon.'

"I used to play my LPs in the dressing room at Bristol until somebody threw the record player out of the window. I never did find out who it was. But it came back in a sorry mess so I took the hint."

"He could be infuriating at times," the late Ron Nicholls said. "You'd be in a tight game of cricket, and he'd be pratting about."

"It wasn't always easy in the dressing room," Arthur Milton recalls. "George Emmett didn't tolerate him as well as he should have done."

"I remember at Taunton once," George's sister Joyce told me. "It was touch and go at the very last minute. Sam Cook was batting, and George was standing, biting his nails. The last over. And Bomber came up behind him and said, 'Boo'. I know George was a great disciplinarian, but he had quite a soft spot for Bomber. He used to make George laugh in spite of himself."

When Bomber is at Nottingham, and Gloucestershire's off-spin is in the hands of Allen and Mortimore, George Emmett seeks him out one day. "'You were a fool to leave,' he told me. 'You were the one I could depend on to bowl a side out.' He was an attacker, you see, like me."

"And did you ever have regrets about leaving?"

"Oh no. The first time I ever went to Trent Bridge I thought, 'I'd love to play here.' The apple and pear trees, the flower boxes on the balcony, the little hut where the ladies used to sell their home-made cakes. You could get there early, read the paper, have a cup of tea and a cake. And the lunches were marvellous, not like the little salads we used to have every day at Bristol, one slice of cold meat so thin you could see through it."

"But what about the cricket, Bomber? Wouldn't you have taken more wickets down at Bristol?"

"Trent Bridge had a bit of pace. It was more enjoyable than bowling on a slow pitch like Bristol. It was more of a challenge to bowl there. Life's nothing if you haven't got a challenge, is it?"

The tea interval is over, and the players are returning to the middle.

"Would you like to buy some raffle tickets?" he asks, reaching into his jacket pocket. "They're for Gloucester City Cricket Club."

A MASTER IN THE TWILIGHT

The evening of the first day

George Emmett has played 24 matches against Yorkshire and, apart from four rained-off finishes, there has been just one draw and that a thrilling one when a young Arthur Milton held out against the wiles of Wardle for 2½ tense hours. "Emmett would rather lose than not try to win," Bomber says.

"We always had good games against Yorkshire," Tony Brown recalls. "Arthur and I were only saying that the other day. I loved playing against them. They were always trying to win. From the word go. They had that Yorkshire instinct, to go out and try to win the match. Lots of other teams wouldn't start from that point. You never had a boring game with them."

"They were the best side for declarations," Bomber says, "because they always fancied bowling you out. They had a tremendous attack, and they encouraged you to have a go."

"We always used to enjoy ourselves when we went down there," Brian Close says. "They were a good competitive lot, the Gloucester lads. Good cricketers."

The Gloucester lads may be a competitive lot, but there are few seasons when they beat Yorkshire. 1948 was one, when George Emmett saved the follow-on with a *'fighting'* 63, then led the most spectacular run chase - 389 in 3¾ hours - with a *'magnificent'* 90. The next success was eight years on in 1956. On a treacherous Bristol wicket, the first three innings of the match produced totals of 95, 88 and 91, at a rate of under two runs an over. Then George Emmett strode out and hit 62 not out in an hour.

"What a great innings!" Bomber recalls, and he is away with another story. "They had this fast bowler, Bob Platt. He took seven for nothing-much in the first innings, and the next morning it was in the paper, how he'd said he could bowl us out with an orange. Emmett was furious. He was so incensed, he smashed him from here to next week. Then when Platty took his sweater, Emmett turned to him. 'How would you like your orange? Peeled or unpeeled?'

"That was the match," Bomber goes on, "when Yorkshire recalled Eddie Leadbeater, the old England leg-spinner. Dear old Eddie, he bagged a pair, didn't bowl in the first innings, then they brought him on with three to win, and Emmett hit his first ball for four. I don't think he ever played for them again."

"George Emmett was a very under-rated player," Tom Graveney says. "He played some wonderful innings."

"Against Derbyshire here at Cheltenham," Bomber recalls. "When they bowled us out before lunch on the first morning. He made 70-odd in the second innings, against Cliff Gladwin, and nobody else got a run." 77 out of 121, Wisden records. "People said that was the best innings he ever played," Gill Emmett says. "He really did get his head down. The tension was horrific. Every time the ball went near a fielder, people gasped. It was very exciting - but very painful to watch."

George Emmett in his prime

"He had this fold-up seat in the dressing-room at Bristol, with a canvas back," Bomber tells, "and he'd sit there with his pads on, waiting to go out to bat."

Then in June 1957, at the age of 44, he hit an *'audacious'* 91 in 67 minutes against the touring West Indians. A small man with strong wrists, he cuts, pulls and sweeps magnificently but, Tony Brown adds, "he could play off the front foot, too. He'd just open the face of the bat and hit it either side of cover point. It was all so effortless."

"He used to wear cotton inners," Tony Brown says. "He'd chain smoke if he was next in, and his gloves would be all nicotine-stained."

"He was quite a worrier really," Gill tells. "He'd give the impression that life was very entertaining, but underneath he used to worry terribly."

"Then he walked out onto the field," Tony Brown continues, "and he walked out as if he was going to take charge right away. But, you know, he must have been out in the nineties more than any other batsman who ever played."

A nervous chain-smoker, so often out in the nineties. It is not what it seems.

"He didn't care when he got into the nineties," Tony Brown reckons. "He just carried on playing his shots. He wasn't going to change the way he played."

"We used to call them the Nervous Nineties," Gill recalls, "but it was us who were nervous. My grandmother, if she was there, she couldn't watch. At the end, I couldn't, either. As soon as he got to 90, I'd go and sit somewhere else. I'd wait till I heard the cheer."

"He threw it away a score of times," Bomber tells. "He tried to get ten in one shot, that sort of thing. He deserved so many more hundreds than he got. Other batsmen played for them, but he didn't. He played exactly the same from start to finish, and they're the kind of people you remember, aren't they? The Boycotts of this game are non-entities. They've given nothing to cricket except facts and figures."

Here at Cheltenham, according to J.M. Kilburn in the Yorkshire Post, his batting is *'delightful, perfectly adapted to the needs of the situation.'* At the Chapel End Johnny Wardle nags away with his flighted slow left-arm, never deviating from his chosen length, but from the College Lawn End the off-spin of the young Ray Illingworth and of Brian Close is less precise. *'He reduced the off-break bowlers to raggedness of length and direction, and he reduced Wardle to agonies of frustration and vehemence of appeal.'*

'Even in the twilight of his career,' the Times reports, *'Emmett is still a master batsman. He punished the slightest deviation of length with wristy pulls and cuts, and was not afraid to hit the ball back over the bowler's head.'*

"He was very, very quick on his feet," Gill says. "I can remember seeing him go halfway down the pitch to hit the ball. These days they never seem to get out of the crease, do they?"

Within a hundred minutes the scoreboard reads 100 for two, but few of the runs have come from Tom Graveney at the other end. Tom is back in favour in the Test team, his 258 at Trent Bridge last month full of *'drives of tremendous power'.* "I was on another last chance, and old Frank Dalling the groundsman saw me when I arrived. 'Don't worry, Tom,' he said, 'I've got a good 'un for you today.'" The Cheltenham groundsman can have had no such words this morning, and this evening *'during one spell from Wardle every ball looked as if it might be Graveney's last.'*

"I was living near Rodmarton," John Light remembers. "I recall taking down a Rodmarton stalwart who'd never seen a county game, a farm worker who played village cricket and worked at harvest time. And the wicket was grim. He came and watched Wardle bowl at Graveney, and he said with great disappointment, because it was the first time he'd seen Graveney, 'Good lord, Wardle makes our Tom look like a bloke batting with a hurdle stick.'"

Johnny Wardle. Tom is back in favour in the Test team, but Johnny is quietly seething at his own exclusion. Last winter Johnny was the hero of the South African tour, 26 wickets in four Tests at an average of 13.80, but he is no sooner back in England than he is making way for his Surrey rival Tony Lock.

"Wardle was a great bowler," Bomber says. "He was a match-winner. And Fred. Two great match-winners. He should have been in the England side for ten years." Ahead of Tony Lock? "Locky threw. Everybody knew that."

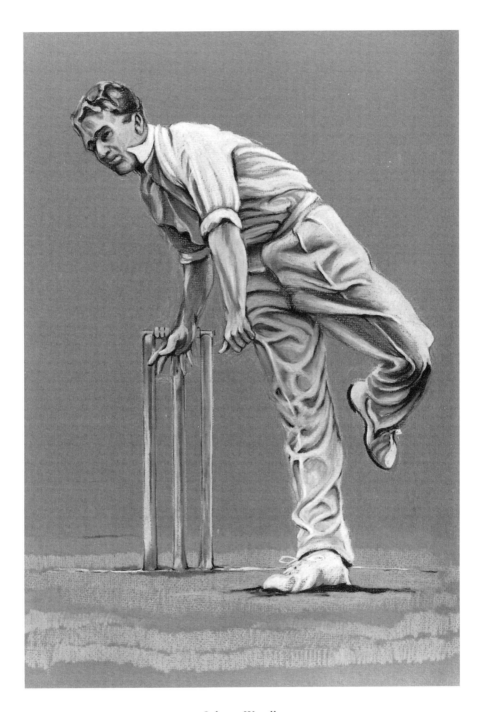

Johnny Wardle

"Johnny?" Brian Close says. "He was the best left-armer in the country at that time."

Last summer at Old Trafford Jim Laker took 19 Australian wickets, the greatest bowling feat in the history of the game, but Godfrey Evans will often say, "If Jim had had Johnny at the other end, he'd never have got so many."

The Reverend David Sheppard scored a century in the same match, and he poses a more startling question. "If Appleyard hadn't got ill, would Laker ever have got back into the England side? Work that out. I think Laker was the best of the lot, but Appleyard was really rather a great bowler."

Laker and Lock, the names trip off the tongue of all England. But it could so easily have been Appleyard and Wardle, and there are plenty of folk in Yorkshire who know it all too well.

Johnny Wardle is bowling slow left-arm here at Cheltenham, in the great Yorkshire tradition of Rhodes and Verity. But on the harder South African wickets he bowled chinamen and googlies out of the back of his hand. The crowds love his comic antics, like the time in the West Indies when he crept up behind the batsman during a drinks break and hid his bat under the matting wicket, or the spectacular catch he triumphantly claimed when the ball had sailed out of the ground. 'Happy Go Johnny' is the title of his autobiography, but those who take the field with him see another side to his personality.

"He looked after himself," Ken Taylor says. "He was a bit of a loner in that way. He would come on to bowl, and he wouldn't try to spin the ball for two or three overs. He'd bowl some maidens, get a good length and line, then when he'd got everything under control he'd start. Whereas Illy and Close would spin it straightaway. But that was part of Johnny's craft. He was a true pro, and he didn't want to give runs away early on."

"I think he was a terribly nervous bowler," David Sheppard says. "It was always thought that he'd liked to have bowled his chinamen more in this country, but I can remember a match when he bowled them at Don Smith and me." It is a game in 1957, three weeks before this one at Cheltenham. "He must have bowled a googly at Don Smith, who hit him for six, and he wouldn't bowl it anymore. I think he was very nervous, very defensive-minded."

"I don't think he was nervous," Bryan Stott says, "but he certainly got some of us on edge in the field."

"He was awful to Bryan in that game," Ken says. "David Sheppard was batting, and Bryan missed an easy catch at short leg. There had been one or two other mis-fields, and he was a bit frustrated. I don't know if it was because David Sheppard was batting, but he sank down onto his knees with his hands in a praying position."

"No, I didn't see that," Bryan says, "but I don't think I'd have been looking in his direction."

In the next match, the Roses match at Bramall Lane, Ken remembers, he bowled his chinamen again at Cyril Washbrook. "Washbrook didn't know if it was

Christmas or Easter. He was playing down the line and missing. He was padding away, and the ball was coming back and hitting him on his behind and all sorts. Johnny was brilliant."

Here on Cheltenham's *'awkward pitch'*, while George Emmett is *'persuading Gloucestershire that their cause is far from lost'*, he is bowling orthodox slow left arm, and he is making 'our Tom' look like a bloke with a hurdle stick. He has 96 wickets this summer, every one of them counted, but, alas, Tom will not provide his 97th. *'Graveney went for a quick second run and was beautifully run out by Padgett, who hit the stumps from about forty yards.'* One old Gloucestershire supporter winces at the memory of it: "In those days Tom had a habit of running with his head down."

Graveney, run out, 22   **Gloucestershire, 113 for three**

"Down at Hove," Ken Taylor remembers. "ten and eleven were in, and I was fielding at mid-wicket. They pushed one just to me, nice and slow, and set off for a run. I picked the ball up and looked at the running end for Johnny to be there. I just had to throw it gently to him, but he wasn't there. So I had to aim at the wicket and I missed. 'Christ, Johnny,' I said, 'you should have been behind the wickets.' And he said to me, 'You don't run nine, ten, jack out.' And he got him out next over."

Mind you, Johnny Wardle is not the only bowler on the circuit with this idea.

"We were playing Notts at Bristol," Bomber tells, "and George Emmett told us to take a chance, get some quick runs. Bruce Dooland was bowling, he'd got about three-for-a-hundred, and Morty ran out Frank McHugh and myself in the same over. And Bruce was standing in the middle of the pitch. 'No, no,' he was crying out, 'don't hit the wicket.'"

Here at Cheltenham Brian Close bowls from the College Lawn End, and George Emmett *'flashed once too often'*, his cover drive ending in the hands of short third man. His innings is over, and he walks back towards the dressing room.

Emmett, caught Pickles bowled Close, 62   **Gloucestershire, 116 for four**

"He'd sit down in his chair," Bomber recalls, "and take his pads off. He'd light up a cigarette, and his hands would be all trembling. He'd sit there for about ten minutes, then he'd come out and watch the game."

The Gloucestershire players sit in their paddock. "If we were batting, we had to watch," Bomber says. "He was a stickler for that. If he came up and asked you how so-and-so was out and you couldn't tell him, you were for it. It was all discipline. I look back now, of course, and I realise the effect. Even when I watch a club match, I watch every ball."

"The best thing you can do as a young cricketer," Tony Brown recalls George Emmett always saying, "is to keep your eyes and ears open - and your mouth shut."

Keep your mouth shut. Not easy for Bomber and certainly not easy for Bobby Etheridge. "He just wouldn't stop talking," Tom Graveney recalls. But what about? "Anything and everything," Bomber says. "Women, mostly."

"That game against the West Indies, when Emmett got 91," Bomber tells. "Sobers was bowling, and he did Derek Hawkins with his quicker ball. Old Emmett was furious. "'Haven't you been watching?' he said. 'Didn't you know he had a quicker ball?' 'Oh yes, I knew,' Derek said. 'I just didn't think he'd bowl it that ball.'"

The match here at Cheltenham could turn once more in the last hour, as Tony Brown passes George Emmett on his way to the middle. It is only in the last six weeks that Tony has had a regular place in this Gloucestershire side, though it is four years since he made his county debut. At Bramall Lane, Sheffield. A nervous seventeen-year-old going out to bat on a hat-trick. "Reg Foord was the bowler. Andy Wilson came in, whistling away, as I went out. 'Good luck, son.' Terrifying. Fortunately he bowled it wide, and I didn't have to play."

'Brown and Milton silenced all fears of collapse and took Gloucestershire into the lead during the last hour.' There are just four wickets down, the lead climbs to 30, and *'there was a drooping of shoulders to be observed in the field.'* Then, just as the picnic baskets are being packed away and the early buses are filling up, Arthur Milton gives Johnny Wardle a late reward.

Milton, caught Binks, bowled Wardle, 18
Brown, not out, 19   **Gloucestershire, 160 for five**

The day is over, and the cricketers retire to the bar.

"We all used to pile in there," Gill Emmett recalls, "and all the players would talk about the day's proceedings."

Martin Young starts with a gin and tonic. "It always had to be Gordon's," Bomber recalls. "When he ordered it, it was like he was making love to the barmaid, and all he was doing was talking about the marvellous Gordon's."

Bomber himself drinks orange squash, but he is as much a part of the fun as the beer-drinkers. "It was lovely playing against Yorkshire when Fred and Closey were young. You'd split up into two parties. Fred would be at one end of the bar, Closey up the other. You could have half an hour of Closey lambasting Fred, then when you got fed up with that you could go and hear Fred lambasting Closey."

Fred and Closey. Each of them is starting the evening with a Pimms. "It was a tradition," Bryan Stott explains, "that, when you won your cap, you had to buy the whole team a drink. Ken Taylor had gone back to football, so I was on my own, and they all had Pimms, every one of them."

Fred and Closey. For all their differences there is a real respect and, in the spring of the year 2000, Brian Close will choose Fred as one of his five cricketers of the century. Then in a radio interview Fred will reveal his five: Donald Bradman, Garfield Sobers, Walter Hammond, Wilfred Rhodes. The interview will last an age as he fires off opinions in every direction. And the fifth? "I'm sorry," he will say. "I've got to go. The dogs are barking for their food."

Outside in the Ford Anglia the Kerry blue terrier waits to be taken home while George Emmett relaxes with a beer and a cigarette. He is 44 now, a survivor from the pre-War days of Wally Hammond and Reg Sinfield, men who played in the best years of Charlie Parker, who first played in 1903 in the heyday of Jessop and the last years of Grace.

"George Emmett was 23 years older than me," Tony Brown says, "but he was still playing. And I learnt so much from him. He gave me my county cap at the end of that summer. 'Well done, Tony,' he said to me. 'I'm giving you your cap not so much for what you have done but for what I expect you to do.' My word, that made me think. I always tried hard, but that made me try even harder."

Tony will play for Gloucestershire till 1976, eight years as captain, then he will become their Secretary. He will give his lifetime to cricket, and he is still on the Committee.

"People don't play to the same age they used to," Arthur Milton says, "and the old boys are not there. We used to learn just as much in the bar afterwards as we did on the field."

County cricket at the start of the year 2000. There is not a player turned forty in the whole country, and the drinks no longer flow all evening.

Sam Cook downs his first pint of beer. The match may not last three days, but the weather has stayed fine and there have been over eight thousand in the ground. The takings come to £843, with another £175 from a collection. The dream of a bungalow looks like coming true.

Let's hope the weather holds till Monday.

A CANKER IN THE ROOTS

Away from the cricket

The Saturday night beer has been slept off, and it is time for the professional cricketers to wake to their day of rest.

A day of rest from professional cricket, anyway. Most Sundays they can be found on a cricket field somewhere in the county, raising money for their beneficiary, and this Sunday they are at the Newlands ground outside Cheltenham, playing a team from Smiths the local engineering firm. A crowd of 2,500 watches Tom Graveney hit *'a sparkling 75'*, then take three wickets with his leg-breaks, and a collection raises £119 - 10s for Sam Cook. A much better day than last Sunday when heavy rain ruined the all-day game at the Duke of Beaufort's Badminton House.

"The Duke of Edinburgh turned out at Badminton one year," Gill Emmett says. "He hit this ball for four. 'Good shot, sir,' they all went. 'Good shot, be damned,' Dad said. 'It was a bloody cowshot.' Then he went in the pavilion after his innings, and the first pint went straight down. It didn't even touch the sides."

At places like Badminton there is always plenty to drink. "When the drinks were free," Bomber tells, "people like Cooky and Youngie used to go mad." Tom Graveney confirms this: "We always knew, if we went on the ground and there were a few tents, we'd be carrying Youngie home."

"I remember one year at Badminton," the late Richard Bernard told me. "Sam got absolutely smashed at lunch and, for some reason I never understood, he was allowed back out onto the field. He wandered around at third man, and he kept appealing all the time and falling over. The crowd roared with laughter. We were bowling down leg so the ball didn't go to him. 'How dare you be so disrespectful to the Duke," Tom Goddard told him afterwards. "You will apologise in person to him.' Poor old Sam was very subdued for a few days after that."

Sam Cook. A Gloucestershire cricketer from 1946 to '64. Then an umpire till 1986. John Arlott calls his television tribute to Sam, 'Forty Years at the Cricket', and Sam contributes a few stories from his playing days. Like the evening George Emmett put him in the slips for a rest and he got hit smack in the face by the ball. 'Don't worry, George,' one team mate said. 'That's not blood coming out of his eye, that's Worthington E.' Or the afternoon he got fed up with fielding in the drizzle at Ashby-de-la-Zouch. "I don't feel too good; I've got a bad tummy," he told the amateur captain Tom Pugh, the only man who never called him Sam. "Go off and have a port and brandy, Cecil. It's the finest thing out for that. And put it down on my expenses." Sam smiles mischievously at the camera. "They came off at seven o'clock, and I was drunk on his expenses."

But there is much more to Sam than his love of beer, and John Arlott spells it out. "I think the Sams of this world are eternal cricketers. I think, although the social background changes, cricketers are cricketers in any generation and in any age. You could go back two hundred years to the days of Hambledon, and you'd find chaps like Sam Cook playing then: philosophical, resigned, not a gambler, not a joker, never chuck a game away, always bowl faithfully and well."

Sam is a craftsman, you see, a plumber in the days of lead piping with individually soldered joints and cast iron soil pipes to be caulked at every collar, not plastic screw-up sections like now. There are no electric drills, only long sessions on a ladder with a bit and brace. If he had bowled better in the Test trial at Canterbury, he might have spent that winter with the M.C.C. in Australia, not negotiating the lanes around Tetbury. "Everybody got snowed in," he wrote in his memoir, "and plumbers were in great demand night and day." There was still snow on the ground in April when he changed his bag of tools for his cricket kit: "I shall never forget getting on the bus with my cricket bag with snow higher than the hedgerows. People looked at me as though I was mad."

Bomber returns to John Bellows the printers each winter, and being a cricketer means nothing there, either. "You just mucked in and had your cup of tea and sandwiches with them. The ordinary working man's got more intelligence than people give him credit for. I don't know about now with all this television, but in those days there weren't the airs and graces. They either liked you or they didn't." And John Bellows himself is a Christian Scientist. "There used to be a sign where you walked in. 'You are entering holy ground,' it said. 'Be careful.'"

Bomber is a machine minder. "The compositors used to reckon machine minders were just comps with their brains blown out." But this is letter-press printing with hot metal, and he recalls the skill of picture reproduction. "All photographs have highlights, mid-tones and solids, and the printer would take a pull, a printed copy. Then he would have another copy done by hand on bank paper and cut out the solids from it and stick them on the pull. So it raised it up. He'd do the same for the mid-tones. It was called making ready. He would stick it on a cylinder with a piece of manilla stretched over, and he would pinpoint where he dug the original pull so that, when he finished making ready, he followed the pinpoints. And then of course they had to set the right amount of ink. I used to watch them for hours, these chaps. They were wonderful.

"Printers were very proud craftsmen. It was the elite trade for years. It's still a very technical business, but now of course the equipment does so much more for them."

August the 18th, 1957. "Cheltenham was the start of the run-down towards the end of the season," Tom Graveney recalls. A fortnight after this match county cricket's round will be over for them all. Sam will take his week's holiday at Bournemouth or Torquay, Bomber on the Isle of Wight. Then it will be back to plumbing and printing.

"I was working on an estate near Rodmarton," Charles Light recalls. "I was in charge of the woods and gardens." His boy John is doing well at Cirencester Grammar School, but Charles has learnt what he knows from experience.

When he retires, he will join the Royal English Forestry Society, and during a tour of the woods at Ebworth he will find himself taking over from the guide. "Ash wants a fur coat and a bare head," he tells the walkers. "Ash on its own is hopeless. You have to put broad leaf, like beech or sycamore, with ash. Ash likes a shaded floor. … There are so many places on the Cotswolds where ash seed blows in and it comes up like winter wheat. … You need to start with fifty per cent larch. Larch, you see, nurses. It draws the ash and the beech up. Then you take out all the larch." But surrounded by so many strange faces he soon stops talking. At the end of the walk, a man comes up to him. "Charlie, why did you stop? I could have listened to you all day. These young people are all piss and wind."

Now there are university graduates tending the woods. Bounced-up book learners, Charles calls them. "A duffer like me, we can only tell things we've proved. Whereas these book people have all these theories.

"I go by local woods now and, dammit, it upsets me. Ash has to be tough. They used it in the First World War for aircraft, didn't they? If you thin it out, it will be beautiful fifty years later. I seem to be the only one now who knows, the only one who bothers."

His own father was Laurie Lee's Uncle Charlie, and 'Cider with Rosie' pays tribute to his work: *The new woods rising are the forests my Uncle Charlie planted on thirty-five shillings a week. His are those mansions of summer shade, lifting skylines of leaves and birds, those blocks of new green now climbing our hills.'*

"Back in the '20s the villages even had a different way of talking from each other. Chedworth had a lovely drawl. North Nibley swore; they put a swear word between syllables. If anybody from Chedworth went to North Nibley to buy a dog, they had to take somebody from Birdlip as an interpreter. And they all looked alike from inter-marriage."

And Tetbury? "They swore quite a bit, too, but they didn't seem to be swearing. It was just their way of emphasising what they were trying to say."

"I should have liked to have done some writing or painting," Charles says. "But I had to leave school to bring home some money. And for years work in the countryside was slave labour."

We are all better off now. "I mislaid my pension book, and they sent me four weeks' worth of giros. Two hundred and eighty pounds. I wish I'd had some of that to give my mother when she was alive."

And we are all worse off. "I haven't seen a lark for years, or a house sparrow. There used to be peewits on top of the Cotswolds, and the hares have got fewer."

He wrote his memories of the countryside for the Stroud News. *'Far below me in the willows by the stream, a nightjar spun his love song to the moon.'* "But they didn't print it as I wrote it. They put 'sang' instead of 'spun', but a nightjar doesn't sing its song, does it?"

Gone are the letter-press printers, making ready. Gone are the old foresters, mixing ash with beech. Gone, too, perhaps, are the old slow bowlers.

At Bristol in the early '50s Charlie Parker passed on to Bomber the wisdom of his 3,000 first-class wickets. "Keep it in the air as long as you can," Bomber repeats. "Up above the eye level. So they can't see it, can't judge it."

But who wants to hear Charlie Parker's words now? "The one-day game got rid of spin bowling," Bomber says. "The coaches and the theorists got this stupid idea that the spinner would be hit out of the ground. And coaches are everything now, aren't they? You watch a good spinner. Viv Richards would murder the medium pacers, but he wasn't at all good against spinners.

"Look at the bowling averages. There are only two decent off-spinners in the country, Saqlain and Muralitharan, and they're leading by many a mile. And we've got this Simon Hughes in the Telegraph saying that there's no future for off-spin bowling. All the batsmen can play it. He says they're freaks. Well, why's Saqlain a freak? Because he bowls a leg-spinner? I used to bowl a leg-spinner. So did Tattersall and Appleyard. He should be asking why our cricket isn't producing bowlers like them. Instead of like him, bloody up-and-down medium pacers.

"You see, people like Simon Hughes weren't born in that era. They can't get to grips with the idea that a spinner is actually a devastating bowler if he bowls well, no matter what the wicket is like. Soon the generation will be gone who remember any different."

"I must say," Tony Brown says. "When I hear Bomber these days, he talks a lot of sense about cricket."

"And back in the fifties? Didn't he talk sense then?"

"He was always talking politics."

"I've always been a member of the Labour Party," Bomber explains. "I remember the 1945 election in Gloucester. All my family were in a big procession right through town. 'Vote, vote, vote for Turner-Samuels, Turn old Boycey out of town.' Sir Leslie Boyce. He was chairman of the Wagon Works, and he knew our dad. In later years, when I played for the county, he came up and introduced himself. I used to print his letter headings at Bellows."

In that election of '45 the Conservatives held Cirencester and Cheltenham, but the rest of the county turned red. Not just the city of Gloucester and most of the Bristol seats but the country districts, too: Stroud, Thornbury, the Forest of Dean.

"When I was in the print at Bellows, I couldn't wait for my sixteenth birthday, then I could join the union. It wasn't because I was active in the union, it was because I'd listened to my father. I had to be in the union. Then of course I mentioned it in the dressing room, because the pay was poor and the conditions were terrible. 'What we need,' I said, 'is a trade union for cricketers.' That's all I said. And there was this deathly hush. The old pros were so traditionalist. They were used to being talked down to, and I was against all that. Within the week, it was all round the circuit that I was a bloody Communist."

Within ten or fifteen years there is a cricketers' union, and the pay and the conditions are transformed beyond Bomber's imagining. But somehow it is not what Bomber wants. "Players like Roly Jenkins, Eric Hollies, lovely people like that had gone, and these new players came in who didn't have that same feeling. Like all sport now, they made it a job of work where we played for the love and entertainment and fellowship."

"Sam Cook never changed," Charles Light says. "For all the people he'd mixed with, he was still Sam of Tetbury, and he'd still got the Tetbury way of speaking. He was very steady, wasn't he?"

There have always been Sam Cooks, John Arlott says in 1986, *'philosophical, resigned, always bowling faithfully and well'*. But can their skills and their characters survive in the world today?

"I don't think I ever saw Sam bowl over the wicket," Arthur Milton says, "like they do now, into the rough. There wasn't a slow left-arm bowler who would lower himself to that. Because it's negative. You can't really get anybody out."

"Did you see when Tufnell bowled that dirty great long hop to that chap who holed out at square leg?" Bomber asks. "When they rushed up to him and cuddled and kissed him. I thought, Sam would have looked the other way if he'd got someone out like that. He'd have felt embarrassed."

"Soon," Bomber says, "the generation will be gone who remember any different." Or, as Charles thinks as he walks through the woods, "Dammit, I seem to be the only one now who bothers."

One day Charles and his wife stopped at Cricket St Thomas where the estate had been turned into a wildlife park. "There was a big beech tree there. I looked down on it from the house, and the innermost leaves were all discoloured. 'I'm going to look round that,' I said to Bess. 'There'll be a white canker somewhere in a crevice between the roots.' And eventually I found it. I knew it had to be there. So I told somebody. 'It's only going to take one strong gale,' I said, 'and that tree will come down.' I was so worried, I wrote them a letter as well.

"But, when I went back the next year, it was still there. So I had another word. 'Mind your own business,' this chap said. He pitched into me; I've never been so told off in my life. 'We've had forestry experts here, and they've assured us the tree is perfectly safe.' The following winter it was on 'Points West'. It had crashed down in the night, onto the roof of the café and the gift shop."

"The theorists have ruined cricket," Bomber says. "It's the funniest, loveliest game under the sun if you just let people get on with it."

"When you hear the word expert," Charles says, "that's when you want to worry."

ON A HAT-TRICK

The morning of the second day

Monday morning. *'Another splendid day for Sam Cook's benefit,'* the Echo reports. Sam's Austin arrives from Shipton Moyne, George Emmett leaves the Kerry blue in his Ford Anglia, and Bomber strolls down from the bus stop. The sun shines, and soon they are all sitting in front of the official photographer.

Standing (left to right): *Harry White (masseur), Ron Nicholls, David Allen (twelfth man), Bomber Wells, Bobby Etheridge, Tony Brown, David Smith*
Seated: *John Mortimore, Arthur Milton, Sam Cook, George Emmett, Harold Thomas (Secretary), Tom Graveney, Martin Young*

"Harry White the masseur," Bomber laughs. "He had hands like gorilla's. He was an ex-matelot. Always smoking. He had the filthiest bloody pipe in Gloucestershire."

"The rub-a-dub man," Tom Graveney calls him. "'Hot and cold, and run it off,' that was always his advice."

"He had no idea," Bomber says. "He came with us because he was cheap. Everything had to be cheap in those days. Just the bare necessities. Big bottle of embrocation, a few plasters, and that was Harry. We used to sneak in behind his back and see the other team's masseur. Dear old Harry. He was a lovely chap. Do anything for you."

Fred Aubrey

There is no sign of the scorer in this year's portrait, but over by the scoreboard on the far side Fred Aubrey is settling to his day's work, laying out his blue and red pens.

"He was a Gloucester man," Bomber tells. "I used to call at his home in Central Road, and we'd walk to the railway station together. He had this watch on a chain in his top pocket, and he was always taking it out and looking at it. Then I met him one evening on the Wagon Works Sports Ground. He was walking his red setter, and I had my cocker spaniel. And we got talking. He'd just retired as a bank manager, he was magnificent with figures, and I said to him we were looking for a scorer. 'Oh, I wouldn't mind doing that,' he said. 'It would be something to do.' And I arranged for him to go down and see Colonel Henson. He was the spitten image of Captain Mainwaring - a short, stout man, fussy. But he was a great little scorer. His books were immaculate."

A bank manager to balance the books. Earlier in the '50s the county had the old off-spinner Monty Cranfield, and his devotion to duty was not like that of Fred Aubrey. "He was rarely in the box," Bomber says. "He'd nip out for a bet on the horses, he'd nip out for a drink. Then he'd come back in and catch up from the other chap."

The newspaper reporters settle in the tent beside Fred Aubrey while the masters of Cheltenham College and their wives take their seats on the balcony of the gymnasium. The best view on the ground. "There'd be 25 or 30 of us," Colin Auger recalls. "Now we're only four or five most days, and we get sandwiched between Severn Sound and the press."

County cricket on a school ground. Northants play at Wellingborough till 1989, a scenic break from their functional Northampton ground, but Allan Lamb and his team mates complain about its low, slow wicket and, until Gloucestershire start playing at the King's School in Gloucester, there is only Cheltenham left.

It is just as well Allan Lamb was not playing at Cheltenham in the '50s. "The wickets were made for the spinners," Colin Auger recalls. "The school played on another square, ten yards nearer the college, and that was a better wicket."

Better for batting, certainly, as Colin will discover next summer when he takes over as cricket master. "We hadn't won a school match at home for about three years. We had a two-day game against Clifton, and on the Friday we got a first innings lead of about 200 and put them back in. The whole school were given the morning off lessons on the Saturday, and that blasted chap Cleese batted from half past eleven to six o'clock for about 30. He just kept plunging his great leg forward. He probably did it on purpose."

Gloucestershire are 160 for five. While they pose for the photograph, the groundsman applies the lightest roller, and Colin and Rosemary Auger settle into their seats. "By ten o'clock there'd be a lot of people in the ground," Colin says, "people wanting to get their favourite seat. Even today you can still see some of the same faces in the same places around the ground."

Monday morning. A working day in the Cotswolds. John Light and his father settle at the Chapel End, and the game resumes. On Saturday the square was damp and green, and now it has dried out. John Mortimore swings Wardle to leg for four, but two balls later he discovers the devil in the wicket. *The ball turned like lightning, to click the bat's edge,'* the Echo reports, and he returns to the pavilion.

Mortimore, caught Binks, bowled Wardle, 4   Gloucestershire, 166 for six

Ray Illingworth sets to work at the College Lawn End and off successive deliveries he removes Tony Brown and David Smith, the youngsters of this Gloucestershire side. Tony advances down the track and is beaten in the flight. Then David pops an easy chance to short leg.

Brown, bowled Illingworth, 19

Smith, caught Wilson, bowled Illingworth, 0   Gloucestershire, 168 for eight

The day is less than ten minutes old, and three more wickets are down.

Now enter Sam Cook. On a hat-trick. In his benefit match.

According to the Times, there is *'a good chance of a hat-trick, too, because Cook is one of those rare specimens, a bowler who has taken more wickets than runs he has scored.'* "I only went in after him," Bomber says, "because he was older than me."

But the Times is wrong. It may say in the News Chronicle Annual that he has more wickets than runs, but in May he altered all that. In that game at Hove, when the pavilion boundary was just thirty yards. In his 12th summer of first-class cricket, he has raised his highest score to 35. It is an innings that his partner that day, Derek Hawkins, will always remember.

"At tea time I was in the middle forties, not out, and George Emmett said to Sam, 'Stick in till Derek gets fifty then give it a go.' I got to my fifty, had a bit of luck, crashed it around, and next thing I'm looking at the scoreboard and I'm 88. Frank Lee was the umpire. 'You can get a hundred here,' he said to me, so I had a word with Sam. 'I'm all right,' he said. 'I'll stick up this end.' They took the new ball, it hit him on the hand, but he still stuck in there. He was great. I bought him a few drinks after that."

"I was at Cirencester Grammar School," John Light remembers, "and the deputy headmaster Frank Miles took assembly. 'A couple of things in the cricket world,' he said. 'Young Derek Hawkins got his maiden hundred for Gloucestershire, and our John Light scored his first fifty for the school. May they both be the first of many!'"

"I was led to the bar to buy drinks," Derek recalls. "In those days you didn't have cheque books or credit cards, you took cash. I was so thrilled, I'd have bought a drink for anybody. I had to phone father to send me some more money."

"Cooky wasn't the worst with the bat," Arthur Milton explains. "He'd try for you. He didn't just have a whack." And Sam will tell you that he scored a century during the war, when he was in the R.A.F. "At a place called Bulawayo," Arthur repeats. "He always used to talk about his hundred at Bulawayo."

The hat-trick ball. But the Yorkshire fielders spread out away from the bat, *'observing the tradition that a beneficiary should not make nought in the first innings of his great match.'* According to the Yorkshire Evening Post, *'Cook made it plain that, with a hat-trick on, he did not expect the usual gift.'*

"The manners," Ken Taylor reflects, "the way the game was played, it was a really super way of playing cricket. I don't see how today you can spend eight hours playing against a team who cheat and shout and scream and then expect to have a nice friendly drink in the bar afterwards."

Sam's offer is declined. *'Illingworth provided a long hop, just outside leg stump, which Cook pushed away for a single.'* Let's hope the game does not hang on that one run. Bobby Etheridge swings the ball to leg for four, but the hope that he will strengthen the Gloucestershire tail is soon snuffed out as he is *'bowled by a ball which came straight through.'*

Etheridge, bowled Illingworth, 4   **Gloucestershire, 173 for nine**

Time for Bomber. The groundsman starts up his roller.

He walks out with a rolling gait, gripping the bat at the bottom of the handle, as if he is stepping out with an axe to chop logs.

"He was pretty agricultural," Gill Emmett recalls. "Sometimes it came off. I can remember him going in and giving it the crash, bang, wallop and scoring quite a few runs. But other times there'd be one crash, one bang, and he'd be out. It was six or nothing with Bomber."

"I only had the one shot," he explains. "The bat went up towards third man, and it ended up at square leg. It was great when it connected."

"He hit two sixes straight off against Glamorgan," Gill's husband Roger recalls. "Into the hospital grounds, where the patients were all sitting out."

'He gives the impression that he's really enjoying himself,' Reg Drury writes in his 'Voice of the West' column. *'And though not everyone will agree - Wilf Wooller also has his disciples - I think that's how it should be.'*

"I remember Wilf Wooller batting for Glamorgan at Cheltenham," Gill says. "He was boring the pants off us all. They started giving him the slow hand-clap, and he sat down on the pitch and refused to go on."

"They were booing and calling out names," Bomber recalls. "So he stopped the game and sat on the floor. It's the only time I've ever been scared on a cricket field.

"Then, when I went out to bat, he turned to Haydn Davies the keeper. 'We only want this daft bugger to hit it for six, and I'll eat my hat.' He was in a right state. I landed it in the gutter on top of the gymnasium. They had to get a ladder to get it down." *'The six of the season,'* the cutting calls it in his battered scrapbook. "So Haydn said to him, 'Do you want salt and pepper with your hat, Wilf?'"

Sam's century at Bulawayo is six thousands miles away, but Bomber's at Stinchcombe is just over the hill. Buried in his scrapbook, the fading pink newspaper, cornered by ancient sellotape, tells the tale: how *'Hurricane Bomber'* came in at 91 for nine and hit a hundred in 35 minutes, with not a care for the reputation of the bowlers. *'When Lancashire's J.H.G. Deighton returned to the attack, he was punched out of the ground first ball.'*

A hundred in 35 minutes. In first-class cricket that is the time Percy Fender took to score the fastest ever century, and he will not have had the delays Bomber had that Sunday. "They must have lost the ball four times. They were building houses next to the ground, and they kept scrambling over this wall into the building site."

Here at Cheltenham he sets about a repeat performance: *'off the mark with a snick to leg'*, *'should have been run out going for a second'* (but "you don't run out nine, ten, jack"), and *'a deliciously rustic six that disturbed the members of the local constitutional club'*. At the other end the fun soon ends as Johnny Wardle bowls Sam Cook. Out for that one single they gave him first ball.

In twenty minutes five Gloucestershire wickets have fallen for 23 runs.

GLOUCESTERSHIRE

*G.M. Emmett	c Pickles b Close	62
D.M. Young	c Trueman b Wardle	13
R.B. Nicholls	c Wilson b Illingworth	1
T.W. Graveney	run out	22
C.A. Milton	c Binks b Wardle	18
A.S. Brown	b Illingworth	19
J.B. Mortimore	c Binks b Wardle	4
+R.J. Etheridge	b Illingworth	4
D.R. Smith	c Wilson b Illingworth	0
C. Cook	b Wardle	1
B.D. Wells	not out	8
Extras	*b 20, lb 11*	31
		183

1-41, 2-52, 3-113, 4-116, 5-160, 6-166, 7-168, 8-168, 9-173, 10-183

Trueman	7	1	23	0
Pickles	7	3	13	0
Illingworth	23	5	65	4
Wardle	24.3	11	29	4
Close	9	2	22	1

A ten minute break. Fred Aubrey completes the balancing of his scorebook by adding up the bowling figures. Illingworth, four for 65 - "I was in my early days," Ray says - and Wardle, the old pro, four for 29.

BOWLER	BOWLING ANALYSIS										Overs	Maidens	Runs	Wickets	Wides	No. Balls
	1	2	3	4	5	6	7	8	9	10						
Trueman												1	23	-		
Pickles												2	13	-		
Illingworth											23	5	65	4		
Wardle											24.3	11	29	4		
Close											9	2	22	1		

But look! The Gloucestershire lead is 50, and 31 of them are extras. The "untidy" Bobby Etheridge, drafted in at the last minute instead of Peter Rochford, conceded none in the Yorkshire innings, but Jimmy Binks - the young stumper who might one day play for England - has let through 20 byes. What has been going on?

John Bapty of the Yorkshire Evening Post talks to Andy Wilson, the old Gloucestershire keeper. "It's a difficult ground for keepers," Andy says. "The ball twists and turns, and it climbs up from the natural turf."

"It was just one of those wickets it was impossible to keep on," Ray Illingworth recalls. "The ball was pitching and rolling."

"No, it never did that at Cheltenham," Tony Brown insists. "We always reckoned that Cheltenham was the best cricket pitch in Gloucestershire. It was never ever low, even when it was wet."

"The ball was taking off," Bomber says, adding his own colour to the story, "going over Binksy's head. So he had a word with Billy Sutcliffe, said he'd stand back. But Wardle refused to bowl if he didn't stand up. And Sutcliffe wasn't strong enough to take Wardle on."

"Jimmy was a great keeper," Ken Taylor says. "He stood up to medium-quick bowlers, people of Caddick's pace, and on wickets that were doing a bit. He always wanted to stand up."

"The ball was keeping low," Ray Illingworth insists. "If you don't stand up, the batsmen just run down the wicket to you. It's a difficult one."

Yorkshire's second innings begins. David Smith and Tony Brown take the new ball, but *they could not repeat the breakthrough of the first innings.* It is a quiet start, three maiden overs, but finally Bryan Stott scores his first run in a Yorkshire cap and, when John Mortimore replaces Tony Brown, *'Watson swept his first delivery into the crowd for six.'* 28 for no wicket, and time for Sam Cook.

Jimmy Binks

"On more than one occasion at Cheltenham," Tony Brown remembers, "the umpire would throw us the ball for the second innings, and we'd play football with it as we walked out. Kick it from one to another, which you can't do now. Maybe you couldn't then, but nobody said anything. Then Sam would rub it in the dirt. Dear old Sam, he always used to rub his hand where his front foot landed, in the soft earth and dust."

Watson has hit John Mortimore's first ball for six. Now Sam's first is short and wide, and he slashes at it. A snick and a catch behind. *'It was a ball which did not deserve a wicket,'* John Bapty writes.

Watson, caught Etheridge, bowled Cook, 14　　　　　**Yorkshire 28 for one**

Doug Padgett soon follows, playing back to a ball *'which hardly left the turf of this natural wicket.'* Keeping low, not flying.

Padgett, bowled Cook, 6　　　　　**Yorkshire, 36 for two**

As Brian Close makes his way to the middle, Harold Thomas, the Gloucestershire Secretary, addresses the crowd over the loudspeaker. "Congratulations," he says. "This is one of the largest crowds ever seen at Cheltenham for an ordinary Monday morning of an ordinary county match." The Echo puts the figure at four thousand, but by the end of the day it will have risen to well over six.

"You walked out," Bomber says, "and there was a buzz of excitement. But once the game was in progress it was so quiet, you'd run in to bowl and you could almost hear the people breathe. Although you don't notice the crowd, it makes a difference when you're playing."

Yorkshire are still 14 behind, and the wicket is growing ever more difficult for batting. For Brian Close, there is only one game plan, and that is attack. He sweeps Sam Cook and is nearly bowled. He sweeps John Mortimore and is dropped by Bobby Etheridge. Then he sweeps Bomber, and *'the mis-hit fell to safety'*. He sweeps him again, this time for four, and at one o'clock the arrears are cleared.

"Closey was my rabbit," Bomber says. "I got him out so many times and always in the most ridiculous ways."

"I know he bowled me once when I wasn't looking," Brian says. "After that I used to tell the others. 'If you don't score off him, get your bat straight back down for the next ball.'"

"The first year I was at Notts," Bomber says, "he had 96 at Worksop, and he glanced this ball for four. We all started clapping, then the umpire signalled leg byes. He stood there cursing away, and he swept the next ball away to leg, and Ian Moore ran all the way round and caught it. Then in the return game at Scarborough he had about 190, and I bowled this long hop down leg. He smashed it away, and Merv Winfield must have run about 40 or 50 yards. He used to run like Charlie Chaplin, feet all splayed out, and he stuck out his hand and caught it."

Brian Close. Nobody in the history of cricket has scored more runs without a double century. "Stamping back to the pavilion," he writes, "cursing myself at every step, I had to pass the hugely grinning Bomber. 'Ah, Closey,' he said. 'Done you again in my leg trap.'"

Here at Cheltenham Bomber delivers another leg-side ball, and Brian Close as ever sweeps. But, according to the Echo, *'he had indulged in the sweep once too often.'* The ball spoons into space on the leg side, and Arthur Milton, *'who used to play on the wing for Arsenal'*, sets off *'like a greyhound'* in pursuit of *'the swirling ball'*. "He ran about forty yards," Bomber tells. "It was the best catch he ever caught, and he caught some blinders." The Yorkshire Evening Post confirms the gist, if not the detail: *'He ran close on twenty yards to make a distinguished running catch.'*

"I had to catch it over my head," Arthur remembers. And was it the best catch of his career? Better than the other 757 that put him in eighth place in Wisden's all-time list? "No, I don't think so," he smiles. "But Bomber would say that. It was off his bowling."

Close, caught Milton, bowled Wells, 10   **Yorkshire, 60 for three**

On the stroke of lunch Bryan Stott pushes out his front pad to Sam Cook. *'A wretched tendency,'* the Times calls it. It is a tendency more fashionable perhaps since Colin Cowdrey won the hearts of all England when he padded away the mysteries of Ramadhin, and *'Stott seemed surprised when umpire John Langridge gave him out lbw.'*

"I do remember that," Bryan says. "I was just playing for lunch. I was lbw, there was no doubt about it, but what a way to get out!"

Stott, lbw Cook, 22   **Yorkshire, 62 for four**

Nine wickets have fallen in the morning. The Cotswold crowd is relishing the prospect of a victory over Yorkshire, but there is little chance now of a third day's takings for Sam Cook.

Yorkshire's lead is just 12 but, as the Times reporter wisely notes, it is likely that a fourth innings target of *'anything more than 100 would take an awful lot of getting on this wicket.'*

Let's get the picnic basket out.

YOU GET THE GIST

Lunch on the second day

"We've got a lovely, juicy melon," Bomber says. "Would you like a slice? … It's a glorious day, isn't it? … Mary, pass Stephen a slice. …

"When I started at Bristol, there was this old boy on the committee, Teddy Spry. As a young man he'd played with W.G. Grace. I used to sit with him. I think I was the only one who did. I loved listening to all his stories. You can learn a lot from old men, you know. They're the obvious people to ask. They might exaggerate things, but it doesn't matter. You get the gist of what they're trying to say."

"You played once with Wally Hammond, didn't you, Bomber ?"

August Bank Holiday, 1951. The county persuaded the great man to return from a five-year retirement, and the young Bomber - three weeks a first-class cricketer - was introduced to him. "It was like standing in the presence of God. You can't describe it, he was such a great legend. He was 48 and looking much older because of the way he'd looked after himself - or not looked after himself. He smiled and shook hands. And I realised what large hands he had, and his forearms were huge like legs of pork. Cooky always used to tell how Hammond lent him an MCC sweater one time, and the shoulders were down on Sam's elbows."

A sad day. George Emmett and Arthur Milton put on 193 for the first wicket. Then, when Hammond stepped out, there was no trace of the old majesty. He was dropped, nearly run out, finally bowled for seven and, Bomber says, "there were grown men weeping when he walked off." "I just sat in the dressing room," Tom Graveney says sadly. "I couldn't watch it."

"Charlie Barnett always maintained," Bomber says, "that Hammond's greatness was that he blinked less than any other person. So he had a clear sight of the ball. You talked to him, and his eyes and eyelids never seemed to move. He just stared at you."

"So what do you think of these five cricketers of the century then, Bomber? The ones in Wisden. They didn't include Hammond, did they?"

"The greatest player who ever lived," Bomber retorts. "I remember Tom Graveney at Chesterfield one year. It was Double Century Week if my memory serves me right. Whoever scored 200 received two hundred bottles of Double Century Beer. Well, Tom got 200 on a green 'un against Jacko, Gladwin and Morgan. The ball was flying all over the place. I was sat next to Tommy Mitchell, the old England and Derbyshire leg-spinner, and I said to him, 'How's Tom compare to Hammond?' And he said, 'He wears white clothes just the same.' 'In style?' I said. 'In splendour?' 'There'll only ever be one Hammond.' He must have been a hell of a player because Tom's innings that day was a beautiful one."

Bomber spent his childhood, sitting on the lino floor, listening to his dad and his uncles talking of Wally Hammond. Then suddenly he was a county cricketer, hearing from the men who played with him.

"Les Ames thought Wally was the most correct batsman he'd ever seen. ... Joe Hardstaff told me that batting with him was like getting a free lesson. ... Andy Sandham said he made him feel second-rate. ... Bobby Wyatt reckoned he could have batted with a walking stick. ... And Reg Perks said that, if he'd had to bowl against him every day, he'd have retired and kept chickens. ...

"Charlie Parker thought he was better than Bradman. I sat next to Charlie at lunch here once, when he was really old and doddery. 'Bradman,' he said. 'He couldn't hold a candle to Wally. Anybody can bat on those bloody wickets in Australia. Wally only had one weakness for a great player: if he didn't feel like it, he wouldn't bother. That was the big difference in their scores.'"

"But Wisden had Hobbs in their five, didn't they?"

"George Cox said to me, 'If you had a car with the two of them getting in, Hobbs would be the one driving and Hammond would be taking it easy in the back. There was no comparison.' What made Hobbs was, he was acceptable to the media in those days. He was a nice, gentle man. A gentleman. Hammond was as hard as nails, a womaniser, a drinker. They are absolutely far out."

"But who would you choose, Bomber, for your five?"

"I would say Greg Chappell, because he proved himself against everyone, whereas poor old Barry Richards didn't. Then I would have whatsisname, the Indian opener."

"Gavaskar?"

"Yes, Gavaskar. What's that expression? *'He's a player who sees beyond the stars.'* Magical. And I'd chuck in Tendulkar as well. They're classical players, aren't they? How they could put Viv Richards in, I've no idea."

"But what about Bradman and Sobers?"

"Yes, I'd have them."

"But that's six, isn't it? Hammond, Chappell, Gavaskar, Tendulkar, Bradman, Sobers."

"Six? Well, I'd have to sit down, and I'd think, who gave the most enjoyment, who had the artistry?" He stops for a moment. "And Bradman would have to go."

Wisden's panel of one hundred yields one hundred votes for Bradman. *'I did wonder if someone somewhere might be contrarian,'* Matthew Engel, the editor, writes, *'but no one dared.'* What a pity he didn't ask Bomber!

"You haven't included any bowlers, Bomber?"

"Bowlers are not entertainers, are they? It's all about batting. Not about bowling. I used to love bowling, just to bowl, but if I went on, or Sam or Mort, and took five or six wickets, we've spoilt the game for a lot of people, haven't we?"

"Barry Richards has been commentating on Channel Four this summer."

"The most natural opening batsman I've ever seen. He was so good, he'd get fed up and get himself out. And there he is on the television now, giving a coaching lesson all the time. He doesn't realise how great a player he was."

"I was secretary at Somerset when Viv Richards was down there," Tony Brown tells. "When people asked me who was the greatest batsman I'd played against, I'd say, 'Sobers was wonderful, but he was an all-rounder. If we're just talking about batsmen, it would have to be Richards.' 'Ah, yes,' they'd say, 'Good old Viv.' And I'd say, 'No, not Viv, Barry.' A lovely player. He always had so much time."

"He's worse than Boycott," Bomber says. "He's got verbal diarrhoea. I mean, you haven't got to speak on television, have you?

"I can talk cricket all day, but all this analysis all the time…. I was listening to Jonathan Agnew on the radio, and he had a New Zealander, a South African and an Australian on. They were talking about this man who was small and used his feet, good at hooking and pulling, and this other man who was six foot two and on the front foot he could do this and that. How you should bowl to the two of them. And I thought, I hadn't been on the staff for a year when old Charlie Parker said to me, 'Never bowl short to a short 'un, never bowl long to a tall 'un.' He said in a dozen words what these four chaps were trying to explain in half an hour. And then they didn't come to any conclusion."

"So you're not a fan of the modern coaching methods, Bomber?"

"It's against my principles to believe in coaching," he says. "I hate regimentation."

Charlie Parker helped out at Bristol in Bomber's early years. A blunt-speaking village labourer's son from outside Cheltenham, he took over three thousand wickets and won just one Test cap. What on earth was it that he said that night to Sir Pelham Warner in the hotel lift? "He never did tell me," Bomber says.

"I asked him one day, 'What do you think of my run-up?' And he reacted immediately. 'Have you got a vest on?' 'No, Mr Parker.' 'Don't come here tomorrow without a vest.'

"'A lot of people think I don't take a long enough run,' I said. And he said, 'You do what you think best. It doesn't matter what you do this end. You can do handsprings and somersaults. It's what happens down the other end. That's all that matters in cricket.

"That's why cricket was such a lovely game in those days. Because you could bat and bowl as you liked. There wasn't the coaching, people had to work out their own methods, so they all had different techniques. The old Lancastrian Grieves, he had a marvellous eye, he'd cut all day: full tosses, half-volleys, good length balls. But now, if a ball comes, they play the expected shot. You can't say to a bowler, 'You aren't bowling the correct way for off-spin.' As long as they do it, that's all that matters, isn't it?

"It's like Everton Weekes said to me, 'Everybody walks differently.'

"Now you've got these lads coming into the game, and their natural instincts are curtailed. They come up as another number. We've taken individuality out of the game and, of all games, cricket has got to have individuality. I think coaches and theorists have tried to make cricket a team game, and it isn't a team game at all, is it?

"I went into cricket. No coaching, self-taught, without a worry in the world. I didn't have any nerves. I just went out and bowled as if I was bowling for Gloucester City on the Spa. 'You're a natural,' somebody said, and I thought, 'What's a natural?'

"I suppose Botham was the last great natural player we've had. He was a man of our times, wasn't he? All rough and ready, but in his heart he was a kind person. People like that, Sobers, Compton, they make it all worthwhile, don't they?

"But these coaches... I think a lot of them are doing it to make money, not to put their hearts and souls in it.

"Everything that they introduce into sport is defensive-minded, isn't it? Instead of getting the batsman out, they give him a single to stop him getting any runs. It's like the body swerve in rugby. Guscott had it, but it used to be everyone. They'd swivel the hips and, woof, off they'd go. Marvellous. But they don't get a chance now, do they? Because it's easier for the coaches to get eight forwards together and train them up to stop it."

"Don Wilson told me of a conversation he had with Peter May when he was Chairman of Selectors," I say. "He was telling Don how they had all these fielders in set areas on the boundary to stop people's shots. 'Peter,' Don said, 'people used to travel miles to see you whip that ball through mid-wicket for four runs. They used to watch you hit that one, bang, through extra cover. They'd leave the ground saying, 'Ooh, that shot of Peter May's.' It'll only be one now, and no one remembers one.'"

"It's easy to defend, isn't it?" Bomber says. "That's why Botham was such a relief. Now it's going through a period when they're struggling to create an audience."

"I think Bomber's right," Tony Brown says. "It is all over-coached. When Tom Graveney or Fred Trueman went to play for England, they didn't have to be told how to play. They didn't have to sit through long sessions about how they were going to bat, how they were going to bowl."

But maybe the standard has gone up. That is what Ben Hollioake thinks. In the Spring of 1998 his brother Adam was captain of the England one-day side, and he himself was already a Test match player. "If we're all honest," Ben told one reporter, "the standard is a lot higher now. I mean, when you watch the old days, like Laker taking all those wickets against Australia, OK they spun a bit, but if Merlin the Magician bowled them today they wouldn't get anyone out. It's truly impossible for those balls to get through a modern defence."

Bomber roars with laughter. "Like when that chap Muralitharan took what was it - sixteen wickets - bowling off-spin against them. They left gates bigger than the Khyber bloody Pass."

The Spring of 1998. Two brothers Hollioake, two new Mercedes, but the old cricketers were not impressed. "The Hollioake brothers," Somerset's Ken Biddulph said to me one day. "I sometimes wonder if in two years' time we're all going to be asking, 'Who were the Hollioake brothers?'"

"Adam scored some runs at Worcester in a Nat-West game," Tom Graveney recalls, "and the Surrey President said to me, 'He'll be playing for England shortly.' And I said, 'If he does, we'll be in terrible trouble.'"

Tom Graveney, 122 first-class centuries and a lifetime in cricket. He admires Graeme Hick, he sees great promise in Vikram Solanki, but he is not impressed by Adam Hollioake. He thinks that the batsmen today pick up their bats wrongly. Do people want his contribution to the game? "They don't let me near the players at Worcester," he says.

But Ben Hollioake, a twenty-year-old yet to make a century for his county, everybody wants his opinions. "People start believing they're tremendously important when they're not," Lancashire's David Green told me. "All these personal interviews, these vignettes of people while they're still playing. 'My views on English cricket, by Ben Hollioake, age 12.'"

The Hollioake brothers. I wonder how they would have developed under the captaincy of George Emmett.

"Cricketers in the last fifteen years," Tony Brown says, "haven't been as enthusiastic about listening to their elders as we were. In those days the disciplines were imposed on young people, the common courtesies. Now young people are taught to question everything."

"It started changing in the Sixties," Bomber says. "The amateurs went out of the game, and these brash young players were coming in, and they weren't playing for the love like we did. All these blokes who bowled seam and could bat a bit. It was a wind of change, and the spinners disappeared like falling leaves. It was a negative way of playing. The amateurs attacked."

He pauses to unpeel a banana.

"It's like that lovely story Charlie Parker used to tell. He was bowling at Ranjitsinhji. And Ranjitsinhji kept glancing him to leg. That was his shot, wasn't it? So Charlie went up to the captain - an amateur, Champain, I think - and he said, 'Excuse me, sir, do you think I could move second slip onto the leg-side to stop him doing that?' And Champain looked at him: 'Good God, man, are you trying to spoil the game?'"

"I look back now," Tom Graveney says, "and I think that the totally professional game hasn't worked out. The good amateur captain and the senior pro were the basis of first-class cricket when I played. The amateur was independent, he took on the committee, and the senior pro handled all the staff. Now they've got the coach, the assistant coach, all these people."

"But in 1957 you were captained by George Emmett, a professional."

"The greatest captain I've ever known in my life," Bomber says. "He'd prefer to lose the game trying to win it than not have a go at all."

I sit and I listen. Bomber, the life-long Labour Party member from the back streets of Gloucester, who yearns for the spirit of the amateur captains like

Champain and Sir Derrick Bailey. Bomber, the happy-go-lucky joker at odds with regimentation, who still admires the fierce discipline of George Emmett and his Kerry blue terrier.

"I used to love to listen to all the old men," he says. "They're the obvious people to learn from, aren't they? They might exaggerate things, but it doesn't matter. You get the gist of what they're trying to say."

The five-minute bell rings.

"Come on, Stephen, have another slice of melon while the players are coming out."

FRED'S NEW BALL BURST

The afternoon of the second day

Yorkshire are twelve runs ahead with four wickets down, and they need an innings of character from one of the two men walking out to the wicket: Ray Illingworth, the canny, young all-rounder, who held their batting together on Saturday, or Vic Wilson, the big, imperturbable farmer who *'has had a sketchy time of late'*. "Vic wasn't a great thinker," Brian Close says. "He played some good innings, but he never altered his style to suit the circumstances." Ray is a right-handed bat, on his way to the season's double of 1000 runs and 100 wickets and counting every one of them. Next summer he will start a Test career that will climax with the England captaincy. Vic is a left-hander who toured Australia in '54/5, but it is two years now since he scored a championship century and he will wait five more years for another one.

'Illingworth was not afraid to use his feet to Cook and he swept him for four, while at the other end Wilson hit Wells through the covers for four to take the score to 70.'

Illingworth and Wilson, the one working out every angle, the other just playing his normal game. Facing Wells and Cook, the one looking for something to happen with each delivery, the other faithfully bowling the ball on the spot. Their umpires today are Dai Davies and John Langridge, and they too are "complete opposites," Bomber says.

Dai is a short Welshman who loves to be part of the action: "He was very flamboyant. He used to boast how good he was - 'If I was bowling against this chap, he'd never get a run.' - and he'd tell you what to do: 'Toss it up a bit, get him to come down the wicket to you.'" He is an experienced Test match umpire, but cricket's folklore remembers him best for the lbw he gave at Bournemouth in August 1948. Glamorgan's John Clay was the bowler, Hampshire's Charlie Knott the batsman, and they say that his finger went up with the words, 'That's out, and we've won the championship."

John Langridge is a tall, quiet man from Sussex, with a red glow around his cheeks. "He looked a proper country boy," Bomber says. "His face looked like he'd just come out of a field with a scythe." A county cricketer for more than a quarter of a century, he is just setting out on another quarter century as an umpire, and he has played against all the cricketers in this match. Not least Bomber.

"Lord's sent out this instruction one year," Tony Brown tells. "There had been complaints so the umpires were to make sure the batsman was ready before letting Bomber bowl. Well, the story in Bristol goes that he was bowling to John Langridge, and John had this long routine. He had to look up, look down, touch his box, look up, tap his bat. And Bomber started to come up, got halfway through his delivery, and the umpire put his arm out. So Bomber just stood there where he'd got to, with the umpire's arm across his chest. John carried on, and the next time he looked up the umpire dropped his arm. Well, Bomber let go of the ball, but John was still going through his routine, and he was clean bowled. 'I'm terribly sorry,' the umpire said. 'I thought you were looking.' 'Well, I probably was looking, but I wasn't ready.'"

The umpires are old professionals. "They would have got better money sweeping up in a factory," Bomber says, "but they loved the game and they wanted to keep it going." Some are old batsmen, others bowlers, and their decisions reflect their sympathies. Ray Illingworth has just come down the wicket to sweep Sam Cook for four, and there is nothing more frustrating for a slow left-armer than to be swept across the line like this. "If I ever become a bloody umpire," Bomber remembers Sam telling him, "I shall have the sharpest finger in the country."

Now Ray faces Bomber, and *'in trying the same tactics, he came down too far and was bowled.'* *'An impish off-break,'* the Bristol Evening Post calls it. In the words of John Bapty, *'the ball was answering the call of the spinning fingers.'*

Illingworth, bowled Wells, 4   Yorkshire, 71 for five

'Once more on this wicket Sutcliffe had to face the threat of anxiety and ceaseless toil.' Two years ago he finished second to Willie Watson in the Yorkshire averages, but that was never going to be enough for the son of the great Herbert Sutcliffe. As if his Christian names - William Herbert Hobbs - are not sufficient burden, he captains Yorkshire at a time when the county's expectations are leading to frustration and impatience and at a time when the outsize elements of the side are not achieving any harmony. "He was a super lad," Brian Close says, "but he was happier having a pint and a natter than he was cracking the whip on the field."

Here at Cheltenham *'for twenty-five minutes he propped while Wilson was copping, and then he was taken in the leg trap.'* A fourth catch in the match for Arthur Milton.

Sutcliffe, caught Milton, bowled Wells, 3   Yorkshire, 95 for six

"It was all right fielding close to the wicket at Cheltenham," Arthur recalls, "but, if you fielded out and about, it was very difficult to see, with all the trees and the college. I remember fielding out at long on to Morty one day, and I think it was Broadbent of Worcester. He used to slice the ball. He looked as though he'd hit it to mid-wicket, and I'm looking at the fielder, thinking, 'When's he going to move?' and all of a sudden there's a shout, 'Arthur', and it nearly hit me on the toes."

Only seven first-class cricketers have taken more catches than Arthur, but "you always remember the ones you drop," he says and he is off with another story, the day he dropped a dolly at Lord's when Middlesex's last pair needed 66 for victory and they got them. "'Bloody brave of you to come in here,' Don Bennett said when I went in the Middlesex dressing room. 'Don,' I said, 'I'm better off in here. They're going to lynch me next door.'"

But then, if you want to find old cricketers to tell you how great they were, don't bother to go and see Arthur. The last man to play cricket and football for England. I interviewed him for my first book, and it was a job to stop him asking me about myself. "When he retired," Bomber says, "Milt could have had any job in the country with his sporting pedigree, but he became a postman. And when he wasn't delivering letters, he was decorating or doing the old pensioners' gardens. He never, ever forgot his roots."

The lead is 45, and the press reckon that *'anything beyond 100 would take an awful lot of getting.'* Johnny Wardle appears, and in a low-scoring match a few big hits from him could turn the contest decisively. Johnny bats left-handed, Sam Cook's turn will suit his leg-side clouts, so immediately George Emmett summons up John Mortimore. *'Wardle hit him straight for four but then missed with two wild swings. He was more selective in the next Mortimore over. He played four of the balls sedately, but he took a lusty couple and a superbly off-driven four from the other two.'*

But the bowling honours today belong to the man the Times correspondent calls *'that genial soul with the shortest run in cricket.'* He has Wardle caught by Tony Brown at short leg. Then Fred Trueman arrives at the wicket. "The easiest person in the world to kid out," Bomber calls him, and by the end of the over Fred is returning to the dressing room. Fred may tell you that his batting average in the Test series this summer is 87, but here at Cheltenham Bomber has bowled him eight balls and dismissed him for two ducks.

Wardle, caught Brown, bowled Wells, 12
Trueman, caught Brown, bowled Wells, 0   **Yorkshire, 115 for eight**

Then Jimmy Binks is stumped off Sam, and Yorkshire are nine wickets down. From the non-striker's end Vic Wilson watches with despair as *'his partners were defeated in variations of ineffectiveness or exuberance.'*

Binks, stumped Etheridge, bowled Cook, 0   **Yorkshire, 116 for nine**

"Bomber was a very astute cricketer," Tony Brown says. "I do remember at Bristol one day. He was bowling, and the batsmen got in a mix-up, a muddle, over a run. The ball was returned to Bomber, and he could have just taken off the bails. Instead, he whistled it down the other end, knocked the stumps out of the ground, and George Emmett went absolutely white. 'Bomber, what the bloody hell are you doing?' He said, 'Well, it's the one at that end we want to get out, isn't it?'"

Vic Wilson has scored valuable runs *'without ever being sufficiently dominant to pick and choose strokes'*, and he makes a last-ditch effort to wrest the initiative, *'attempting to clear the school pavilion'* and being stumped by Bobby Etheridge.

Wilson, stumped Etheridge, bowled Wells, 45   **Yorkshire, 118 all out**

Etheridge and Wells. They have replaced Peter Rochford and David Allen, and they have had a great day. Bobby Etheridge has cleaned up the innings with two stumpings, and he has conceded just two leg-byes on an awkward wicket. Bomber has six wickets in the innings, eight in the match, and he leads in the team. Gloucestershire need 69 to win, and *'a fine crowd were saying some unflattering things about the appearance of the White Rose at Cheltenham.'*

YORKSHIRE

W.B. Stott	lbw b Cook	22
W. Watson	c Etheridge b Cook	14
D.E.V. Padgett	b Cook	6
D.B. Close	c Milton b Wells	10
J.V. Wilson	st Etheridge b Wells	45
R. Illingworth	b Wells	4
*W.H.H. Sutcliffe	c Milton b Wells	3
J.H. Wardle	c Brown b Wells	12
F.S. Trueman	c Brown b Wells	0
+J.G. Binks	st Etheridge b Cook	0
D. Pickles	not out	0
Extras	*lb 2*	2
		118

1-28, 2-36, 3-60, 4-62, 5-71, 6-95, 7-115, 8-115, 9-116, 10-118

Smith	6	3	10	0
Brown	4	1	8	0
Cook	17	8	28	4
Mortimore	15	6	27	0
Wells	21.5	8	43	6

It is half past three on the second afternoon, and already the match is entering its final innings. There will certainly be no third day takings for Sam Cook. "When we came off," Bomber remembers, "Sam's committee were all in the dressing room with these buckets. 'Get round quick,' they said, and off we went around the ground."

Meanwhile as they walk out to the middle the Yorkshire team is debating its tactics. Should they open with Fred Trueman, England's number one fast bowler, or should they rub the ball in the dirt and turn straight to Wardle and Illingworth? They would not be Yorkshire if there were not plenty of opinions expressed, and their opponents love to dwell on the apparent disharmony.

"Fred wanted to show people how good he was, that he was the boss," Bomber tells. "He insisted on opening the bowling, and Billy Sutcliffe let him. If Sutcliffe had had any sense, he'd have opened with the spinners. In a way, he did exactly what Basil Allen did in 1947." How that Middlesex match still haunts the memories of all Gloucestershire! It was their greatest chance of winning the championship, it was a turning wicket, and their captain B.O. Allen let Middlesex make 62 before Tom Goddard bowled a ball. "All his life, Basil Allen told me, he could never work out why he hadn't brought him on earlier."

"Fred should never have been given the ball," John Light says. "Sutcliffe probably knew that, but he wasn't strong enough to keep it from him. Apparently Fred said, 'I'm the England fast bowler, you can't not use me.'"

Fred Trueman

"No, it wasn't like that at all," Ray Illingworth says. "George Emmett was a very good sweeper of off-spinners, and we didn't want to risk giving any runs away like that. That was the reason. I can assure you of that."

As Fred marks his run-up from the College Lawn End, George Emmett struts out to the middle. "Cricket provides such a great stage, doesn't it?" Bomber says. "Cardus said it was worth your entrance fee just to see Hammond walk to the middle." *'In this sulphurous moment of crisis he walked down the pavilion steps of Lord's like the Queen Mary gliding down the stocks to a flowing sea.'* "I think Emmett secretly was a bit of a show-off, too. He loved to shine, to outplay Gravy or Milt or Youngy, to play shots they couldn't play. And, with Fred bowling and the press all full of Fred's exploits, he'd have wanted to take him down a peg or two."

For many cricket historians George Emmett has just one Test failure, to the pace of Ray Lindwall, to show for his career, and one writer, Derek Birley, even refers to the 'lunacy' of Len Hutton's being dropped in favour of 'a very ordinary county cricketer'. It rankles with his family still, but they preserve their scrapbook and their own memories: his 141 at Bristol when Lindwall and Miller returned in 1953 - "the two-fingers job," Gill calls it. "I guess he felt that honour was satisfied." - and the 91 in 67 minutes earlier in this summer of 1957 against the West Indies: "A wonderful innings," Tony Brown recalls. "You couldn't better it." He will retire at the end of next summer, but he will be back at the age of 46 in 1959. His last innings on Gloucestershire soil will be here at Cheltenham against the touring Indians: 85 in an hour and a quarter, *'a lesson in brilliant stroke play'*.

The annual tourist match. In the days before overseas players and television, there is no greater stage to show what you might have done if you had been playing for England. George Emmett toured India twice with a Commonwealth eleven, and his team mate Frank Worrell had no doubts about his ability. "He was one of the greatest batsmen I have seen in the tropics," he told the Daily Express in 1965. But then George was a boy in India, and family legend even has it that he was dragged off by a tiger and only saved by his grandmother's shouting. "I think that was probably apocryphal," Gill says.

"He was curry mad," Bomber recalls. "He took Morty and me for an Indian meal in Oxford once. Never again." Gill smiles: "My father could eat curry that was so hot you almost couldn't taste it."

He strides out to the wicket to face Fred. A boy who grew up in a land of tigers, a cricketer who suffered the put-downs of Wally Hammond, a soldier who fought in the desert. He is a professional captain, but not for him the dour no-risk cricket of the next generation of professional captains. "I was told that one of my troubles was that I had too many strokes," he will say in 1961. "If I couldn't get a bowler away, I'd always try another way. But today people don't take the risks. Shots that were termed good before the war are now termed risky."

Fred Trueman to George Emmett. This is cricket that will stay in the memory.

"I can see Fred now," Bomber says. "He had this white shirt on, blowing in the wind of a lovely afternoon and, when he strolled back, you could see all his muscles straining. Crikey, what a wonderful sight! I can see him now, rolling up his sleeves, and coming in with that beautiful action. And I can see Emmett stood there, regardless, and he took him on. First ball he hit him through the covers. A magnificent shot." *'The loveliest stroke of the day,'* the Times calls it. "Of course for Emmett there was glory in that."

Four for no wicket, and Fred returns to his mark. "Sometime during that over," John Light recalls, "he ran across to where the bucket was going around for Sam Cook and made as if to throw some money into it. Then he went back and bowled the next ball." Fred is a showman, trying to prove that he is the boss. By the end of his two overs he has conceded 12 runs, two leg byes and four byes down the leg side. Gloucestershire are 18 for no wicket, and over a quarter of their target of 69 has been knocked off. *'Wardle rubbed the shine off the new ball, and Illingworth joined him in the attack.'*

George Emmett loves to attack the off-spinners, and to Illingworth's fourth delivery he is down the wicket and hitting the ball hard to leg. "He swept at me," Ray recalls. "Vic Wilson was at short leg, and it hit him on the boot and bobbed up in the air." Yorkshire, afraid of what Emmett will do to Ray, have given the new ball to Fred, he has cost them eighteen runs, and now Ray has trapped him without his adding to the score.

George Emmett has seen off the great Fred, an innings Bomber will always remember, yet he returns to his Players' Medium cigarettes with just a handful of runs to his name.

Emmett, caught Wilson, bowled Illingworth, 6   Gloucestershire, 18 for one

From the Chapel End Johnny Wardle has opened with three maidens, and now he is *'turning the ball encouragingly or alarmingly, according to the point of view, but sharply to any eye.'* Martin Young tries to pull him into the gymnasium, but he skies a catch. Then Ron Nicholls edges to the keeper. *'The first seeds of worry were planted in the minds of Gloucestershire supporters.'*

Young, caught Stott, bowled Wardle, 9
Nicholls, caught Binks, bowled Wardle, 7   Gloucestershire, 30 for three

Tom Graveney. Not only has he scored more runs in the last three summers than anyone else in England but he has scored them with style and elegance and on wickets that modern players could hardly imagine. "Gravy was a magnificent player in his Gloucester days," Bomber says. "People said he was a better player when he went to Worcester, but I said, 'No, no, not half the player.' First of all he's batting at Worcester, one of the most beautiful wickets in the world, not on our sand heaps and little shooting pitches. Secondly he cut out so many of his shots to make himself an England player again. At Bristol in those days he was an attacker."

Arthur Milton is not so sure. "You were never able to dominate on our pitches. So it took away your attacking instinct. If we had had good wickets, I don't think Tom would ever have been out of the England side. Bradman played at Bristol in 1930, and he never played there again, did he? I often wonder what the record books would be like if Tom had grown up in Bowral and Bradman had had to play his cricket at Bristol."

Tom draws the parallel between himself and David Gower. "I always felt so sorry for David. He was stylish, elegant, and, if you play like that, every time you miss the ball and the stump flies out, everybody says, 'What a bloody casual shot!' But if that's the way you play, you can't do anything about it."

Style and elegance. As one historian has written of Tom, "The man and his batting were made for the lovely Cheltenham ground." But alas nobody's batting is made for the Cheltenham wicket as it has become today. The ball is shooting, and Johnny Wardle is at his teasing best.

Ray Illingworth is bowling towards the Chapel, where the wicket is playing a little easier, and Tom hits him to leg for four, then runs a single. But at the other end, facing Johnny Wardle, the problems are almost insurmountable.

"I do recall Graveney facing Wardle after getting a couple of shooters," John Light says, "and he took guard with his bat horizontally along the crease, smiling down the wicket." *'Wardle certainly made the ball move, and he had Graveney hopelessly tied up.'*

"I was walking round with a bucket for Sam," Bomber recalls, "and people started saying to me, 'Go on, Bomb, you'd better get them on, you're going to be wanted.'"

With tea only minutes away, there is a gasp from the crowd. *'As always seemed likely, Graveney got an edge and was well caught low down at slip.'*

Graveney, caught Wilson, bowled Wardle, 5   Gloucestershire, 35 for four

Arthur Milton manages two singles, and they all leave the field. According to the Times, *'every West Countryman in sight had retracted anything disrespectful he had said of the northern foe.'*

Milton, not out, 2
Brown, not out, 0   Gloucestershire, 37 for four

Time for the picnic basket.

Time for another natter.

THEN AND NOW

Tea on the second day

Gloucestershire are 37 for four, struggling to score 69 on a difficult wicket. Another Cheltenham match that will be over in two days.

But move forward to Cheltenham in 1999, to four-day cricket on a flat, batting track, and Worcestershire have declared at 591 for seven. Weston 139, Hick 122, Solanki 171. "This Solanki, he's like Pataudi, all wrist-work and timing," Bomber says. "He could go to the top." Between them Gloucestershire's two off-spinners, Ball and Snape, have taken two for 224. "Bally's just putting it there. He needs to get his front foot across more, bowl across his body. There's no rotation. He's just lobbing it in there, not bowling it."

Time for a slice of cake.

"You want to get yourself announced on the tannoy," he tells me. "Say you'll be signing copies of your books in the club shop after tea."

"No, I don't think so, Bomber."

"Go on," he says, slapping his hand on the arm of his wheelchair. "They'll be queuing up for you. I'd announce it myself if I could walk over there."

A round-faced man, with a bright blazer and a panama hat, appears. "Bomber, how are you?"

"Martin." Martin Horton, Worcestershire's off-spinner in the 1950s. "Pull up a pew, my friend. Would you like a cup of tea?"

"No, it's all right, thank you."

"Mary, pour Martin a cup of tea. We were only talking earlier about dear old Roly Jenkins. Were you playing here that day Emmett kept hitting him for four? 'Emmett, if you don't like me,' he called out, 'that's fair enough, but for God's sake don't keep taking it out on the ball.' And everybody laughed. You couldn't do it now, could you?"

"I remember him down at Bristol once," Martin says. "He was inspecting the pitch. 'Look at all the sand,' he said. 'I'd have brought the family and the deck-chairs if I'd known.'" In 1956, perhaps, when Sam Cook had match figures of ten for 35 in 45 overs.

My cricket writing began when I was going up to Stroud each week for a net with Ken Biddulph. I loved to stay on and listen to his tales of cricket at Somerset. So I asked him to tell me the story of his most memorable match; I thought it might make a magazine article. "I'd be delighted," he said, and he chose a game at Bath when Somerset beat Yorkshire for the first time for 56 years. *'Yorkshire were a hard team to play,'* he began. *'The atmosphere was always a bit different. They had this self-belief. When you went in to bat, they used to look at you as if to say, 'How dare you come out here!' They could not be beaten.'*

"I'm wondering if I could do a whole book like this," I said later. "What other old cricketers would be good to interview?"

"Martin Horton," he replied, quick as a flash, and two weeks later I was sitting in Martin's front room. "The only trouble," he said, "is that I'd also like to pick a match when we beat Yorkshire." By the third interview I was wondering if the book should be 'The Day We Beat Yorkshire'. It seemed to be every county cricketer's most vivid memory. "No, if you don't mind," I'd say, "perhaps you could choose another match. Do you remember any good games against Kent?"

"Excuse me," a middle-aged man says, hovering beside Bomber and Martin. "Would you mind signing my autograph book?"

Martin signs, then Bomber, who gestures to me. "Don't forget Stephen here. Author of the best two books on cricket ever written. You'll want his autograph."

What was it Bomber told me? "When I first started, old chaps used to come up to me at Bristol, and they'd tell me how I was better than Tom Goddard. But I don't think they really meant it. I think they were just trying to build up my confidence."

The autograph-hunter stares suspiciously at my signature and turns back to Bomber and Martin. "I reckon you two would walk into the England team if you were playing today."

What fun it is to make these comparisons!

I sit and listen to them talking, and nothing they say seems to fit with what I read in the papers.

'We play too much in this country,' everybody says now. But, in the 1950s when England had the best team in the world, they played every day all summer.

"There's no way I could play now," Tom Graveney says, "because I wouldn't bat often enough. I wanted to bat every day. I was getting a rhythm. When you get a rhythm, you don't have to think when you get out there. I don't think they play often enough now."

"One year," Martin Horton recalls, "I had 60-odd innings in first-class cricket and still bowled about 800 overs. You thought nothing of it." 66 innings, 896 overs, in 1961, and he will have played benefit matches most Sundays as well. "Come August, you'd think, 'Not long now', but a couple of weeks into the winter you'd be missing it."

"You can't play too much," Bomber says. "The more you play, the more skill you develop, the more experience you've got. I never ever heard a bowler in my day complain of bowling too much."

In the summer of 1997 a 30-year-old Angus Fraser, fresh from a winter off, bowled in all but one Sunday match in Middlesex's programme. 752 overs in all cricket in a 22-week season. He is 'Mr Reliable,' according to Jonathan Agnew: "He has earned his reputation through sheer hard work." Yet in 1962, a 37-year-old Derek Shackleton, off a similar run, bowled 1717 overs in just 17 weeks. "That's what I was paid to do," Derek says.

"It wasn't work," Bomber says. "If you can play the game, cricket is as simple as falling off a log. But if you have to be trained to play it, that's when it becomes hard work."

But today's players, what do they think? Wisden Cricket Monthly lists the ten most common opinions expressed in 'The Cricketers' Who's Who 2000', and second on the list is, *'Too much cricket is played, and there is not enough time for preparation and training.'*

'Four-day county cricket will improve our best players,' they say now.

But Tony Brown does not agree. "The guys today don't understand," he says. "They say that four-day cricket will give them time to score their runs. They want to play on good pitches so they can score 150 in a day and a half. It's a load of nonsense. The art of batting is to score your runs at optimum speed. With three-day cricket, if you played on a good wicket, you'd look to have 350 on the board just after tea so that you'd got time to bowl the opposition out. But if the pitch wasn't so good, you scored as many as you could, and, if somebody got 50 out of 120, they'd played a wonderful innings."

"When you look at people's records," Arthur Milton says, "you have to take them with a pinch of salt. Averages don't tell you the state of the game. I liked nothing more when I was batting at number five than for three wickets to be down early. It would really sharpen my concentration."

"Three-day cricket brings in the art of captaincy," Bomber says. "The art of declaration, the art of bowling a team out, especially on uncovered pitches where a spot of rain might change everything. But now it's like Parkinson's Law, isn't it? The players are only achieving in four days what we used to do in three. And they don't think a thing about the general public. It isn't the length of time, it's what you do in the time that matters."

Four-day cricket. If the two sides in this 1999 match had bowled their overs at the same rate as in the 1957 match, they would have reached a result at the end of the third day, not at five o'clock on the fourth evening.

What do the players of today say to that? There in their top ten opinions, *'There should be fewer overs per day in the Championship'* and *'Intervals, particularly tea, should be longer.'*

'The batsmen won't improve until we make better pitches,' they say, and I compare this run feast here in 1999 with the low-scoring game in 1957.

"Wardle's making our Tom look like he's batting with a hurdle stick," John Light's friend says, but in his next innings 'our Tom' will be the star of the Oval Test, hitting 164 *'with splendid stroke play'*. "The pitch at Cheltenham was terrible," he says, "but I think the modern day players miss a lot of fun. We played on wet pitches, where the ball turned and bounced, so we really had something to work for."

"They wouldn't start today on a pitch like that," Bomber reckons. "But in my day the captains always wanted to get out and play. I remember one time at Bristol. It was raining and raining, and Sir Derrick couldn't be convinced that we couldn't get some play in. He went out to inspect the square with the groundsman's wellingtons on. Laugh? We burst out laughing. But he didn't bat an eyelid.

"Of course, if you did get out and the run-ups were wet, the spinners bowled till they dried out. Now it's all covered, and they've put down all these fertilisers, and it only seems to help the seam bowlers. The ball's still shining after 85 overs."

"People make too much fuss about wickets now," Geoff Edrich says. "The cricket was far more interesting on uncovered wickets, with far more spinners. As soon as the ball does something now, they're in trouble. They haven't got the technique; they don't move their feet correctly."

Here at Cheltenham Graeme Hick makes an easy century but, when he returns to Test cricket, it is on an Old Trafford wicket with a low bounce and he *'got his bat and feet tangled and was lbw to a full toss.'*

So what should we conclude? That his technique is not as developed as it would have been forty years ago, or that the Old Trafford wicket is a disgrace?

Peter Robinson works with the young players on the Somerset staff. "They go off to play club cricket, and they come back with nothing much. 'The wicket wasn't any good,' they say. Or 'the umpiring was useless.' Well, that's always been the case. My uncle was Roly Jenkins. He always taught me to have respect for any cricket."

"It's not just the batsmen," Bomber says. "When you bowl on a bad pitch, you've got to be a good bowler. You have so many close fielders. You can't afford to bowl halfway down the wicket. And you've got to make the batsman play. Nowadays, even in Test cricket, you see them bowling three or four balls outside the off stump, and the captain is at first slip, clapping. If I'd done that, George Emmett would have put his boot up my backside. I used to apologise to the batsman if I bowled a ball he didn't have to play."

"People say we're not competitive enough," Warwickshire's Tom Cartwright told me. "On uncovered pitches you had to compete almost all the time. And if you survived, you learnt."

"If you're a natural player," Bomber thinks, "you can adapt to any pitch. It's only the lesser players who struggle. Since the pitches have been covered, the players haven't served a proper apprenticeship in the game, have they?"

Bomber was seven years an apprentice printer. "B.O. Allen used to say it took five years to become a good county bowler, six years a batsman. 'Just like an average apprenticeship,' he said. You learned by doing the job."

And the cricketers of 2000? *'Pitches need to improve'* and *'They should be prepared by centrally-contracted groundsmen.'*

'We need to catch up with the more advanced coaching methods in the world,' people say now. 'The game's moved on, and we're being left behind.'

But Arthur Milton does not agree. "There's far too much coaching," he says. "Take batting. First thing you've got to do is to have an eye for the ball. Then you've got to defend your wicket. It's as simple as that."

"All this bloody stupid coaching," Brian Close says. "They've interfered so much with the game, it isn't true."

So what coaching would the old players like to give?

"Nobody in this country holds the bat properly," Tom Graveney says. "All the top hands have gone around; nobody plays up and down anymore. When you watch these replays, they're only playing with half a bat."

They wonder why swing bowling has disappeared from this country," Tony Brown says. "It's only disappeared because all the so-called experts want the bowlers to whack the ball in halfway down the wicket. You don't see McGrath waste his time bowling like that. We go on about the Australians. There's nothing superhuman about them. They just do the basic principles awfully well, that's all."

"Coaches have spoilt cricket," Bomber says. "They haven't made it better. In our day, the coaches helped you when you were having a bad spell. They didn't dictate to you. Some of these kids now are like robots."

"County cricket is all very matey and lovey-dovey," England's captain Nasser Hussain says. "No one is sledging anyone. We have got to get a bit of nastiness into our game."

I met Geoff Edrich, and he told me about his first-class debut at the Wagon Works ground in Gloucester in 1946. "I'd been given lbw against the Home Counties when I'd hit the ball, and I thought I was lucky to get another chance. I got to about 20, then I played forward defensive to Tom Goddard and got a faint tickle onto the pad and up to short leg. Tom Goddard shouted, a terrific appeal, and the umpire gave me not out. Wally Hammond was first slip. At the end of the over he walked down the pitch, swinging his arms like a prince. And he didn't look at me. He just walked, and I heard the voice, 'Your brother Bill wouldn't have done that.' So I got to the other end, waved my bat at one from George Lambert, and the castle went down. I just wanted to get out. I wanted a tunnel. From that day forward I never stayed when I got a touch."

How soft, the modern players think.

Geoff appears in 'Runs in the Memory', facing Frank Tyson at his fastest on an Old Trafford wicket that was as rough as they come. Early in his innings his hand was broken, and it was hit several times more while he made 81 out of 141. Back in the pavilion he pulled off the glove and, I was told, "his hand looked as if it had been hit repeatedly by a two pound hammer." But then this was a man who had spent over three years on the Thailand-Burma railway, whose weight had been down to six-and-a-half stone, and who had returned to England to find that his wife had long presumed him dead.

Were they soft, these men after the war?

Or were they the hard ones? Living without all today's comforts and conveniences. Working hard to reconstruct a Britain in which there was such a thing as society, in which there was public service, in which the playing of sport was more than the making of money.

Perhaps it is today's sportsmen who are soft. And soft not least because they think that you can't be hard and competitive without being nasty and cheating.

"I was watching Chelsea on the television last night," Bomber told me one day. "This chap came on, and he pretended he'd been tripped up, got a penalty. 'That's what I like about him,' the commentator said. 'He makes things happen.' Well, he'd cheated, that's all. And we're bringing the children up to think that that's how sport should be played."

Arthur Milton sighs. The last man to play both cricket and football for England. "All the romance has gone out of sport, hasn't it?"

Then and now. Has the world moved forward? Have we taken the best of our past and created a better present? I wonder.

"Have another slice of fruit cake, Stephen. I don't think I'd get to play these days, would I? Not with my waist-line."

Let's get back to 1957. A large crowd is buzzing with the excitement of a tense finish. Some of them are restive for Bomber to appear and slog a couple of sixes. Happy times!

TEN TO MAKE AND THE MATCH TO WIN

The evening of the second day

Emmett, Young, Nicholls and Graveney are out. The ball is turning sharply for Wardle and Illingworth, and five fielders cluster menacingly around the bat. "The art of cricket," Brian Close says, "is in the field, getting the other side out," and he holds *'a quick slip catch'* off Wardle to remove Tony Brown. Then John Mortimore, *'who has played determinedly'*, drives Ray Illingworth, only to see the bowler take *'a fierce chest-high catch.'* An hour ago a Gloucestershire victory seemed a formality, but now the crowd is in a state of great excitement: *'silent at the fall of each wicket, in noisy raptures over every run.'*

Brown, caught Close, bowled Wardle, 0
Mortimore, caught and bowled Illingworth, 2   **Gloucestershire, 46 for six**

There are still over twenty runs needed, and one look at the bowling figures is enough to show what a mountain is still to be climbed:

Wardle   *14 overs, 8 maidens, 4 wickets for 12 runs*
Illingworth,   *13 overs, 5 maidens, 2 wickets for 14 runs*

What a wonderful bonus those two overs from Fred Trueman - 12 runs and 6 extras - must now seem.

With Bobby Etheridge coming to the wicket - *'the last with serious claims to understanding the arts of batsmanship'* - the main responsibility lies with Arthur Milton, who has *'defended grimly for over half an hour.'* "He played very well that day," Tom Graveney remembers. "He was a wonderful player on spinning pitches. He used to play off the back foot, watch it onto the bat, where I used to be on the front foot."

"Milt would go right back," Bomber says, "and he'd follow the ball like a snake. I know Tom was always on the front foot, he even hooked on the front foot, but too many players now are coming forward. If you've started back, it's easy to go forward. But if you're forward, you can't go back, only to where you started from." Or, as Bomber's 'Keep It Simple' Coaching Manual would say, "You can go from A to B, but you can't go from B to A."

"If Arthur had had a little bit of devilment in him," Tom says, "he would have been a hell of a cricketer."

"He never used half his talent," Bomber reckons, "but the half he did use was marvellous."

And Arthur, what does he say? "I

played because I loved it. I think it was born in me to play. I didn't make any money, but I was always happy."

He is joined at the wicket by Bobby Etheridge. Another all-round ball player but one with a very different temperament from Arthur. "I can see Eth now," Bomber says, "sitting in the dressing room, waiting to bat. A tall, fair lad, all skin and bone, but he wanted to get out there. 'Let's get them,' he was saying. He had no fears at all. He was another natural, though, wasn't he? Your natural players are always the best." According to J.M. Kilburn in the Yorkshire Post, *'Etheridge took a line that might reasonably have been expected earlier.'*

From the Chapel End Johnny Wardle starts the 30th over of the innings, the scoreboard reads 47 for six, and off the second delivery *'an old-fashioned swing by Etheridge'* sends the ball for six on the short gymnasium side.

Johnny Wardle. Last winter he was the great success of England's tour of South Africa. "A great bowler," Bomber says. "A match winner." Here at Cheltenham he has taken four for 12 off fourteen overs, and now Gloucestershire's reserve wicket-keeper has swung him away for six. "Names didn't bother Eth at all," Arthur says. And Johnny Wardle? "He was somewhat taken aback, but I said to him, 'Don't worry, Johnny. He wouldn't even know who you are.'"

The scoreboard now reads 53 for six, and to the next delivery Bobby Etheridge swings again, *'clearing slips' heads for another three runs.'* In two balls he has overtaken his partner Arthur's half-hour score, and *'the unashamedly biased crowd were in pandemonium.'*

"Some players rise to an occasion," Bomber says. "Eth certainly did. His type was a dying breed, with his 'devil may care' attitude."

They are on the attack for the first time since George Emmett took on Fred's first over, and Arthur feels the pressure lifting. "I thought, we'll get home now." The next ball is bowled, the fourth of the over, and he joins in the fun with *'a violent cut'*. "He bowled me a short one," he remembers. "I hit it right in the middle of the bat, and Closey in the gully turned away and it hit him on the back." *'Slips and gully made instinctive retreat in self-protection, Close was hit, and the ball fell within Trueman's grasp for an incredible catch.'*

Milton, caught Trueman, bowled Wardle, 8   Gloucestershire, 56 for seven

"Go on, Bomb, you'd better get them on," the crowd called out when Bomber was taking round the bucket, and now he emerges to their delight. *'A little belatedly,'* according to the Echo. A couple of his sixes, like the ones here against Wilf Wooller's Glamorgan, and the match will be over. He scored 42 in 23 minutes that day, and there are only 13 to win now.

Bomber loves to tell the story of that innings, how Wilf Wooller threatened to eat his hat and how they then had to fetch the ball out of the gutter of the gymnasium. But Arthur Milton's memory of Bomber's batting runs more easily to another Glamorgan match: at Newport in 1956, the day Tom Graveney scored 200 out of 298 on a pig of a wicket. "I put on about 120 with Peter Rochford," Tom recalls, "and I think he only scored about 13 of them. And when I came off, I heard this voice behind me. 'That's the worst bloody 200 I've ever seen.'" He laughs: "Wilf."

So what was Bomber's part that day? "We used to take the train to Newport," Arthur explains, "and we only had to walk over the bridge to the ground. The train back used to leave just after seven, and it was nearly ten to when Bomber went out to bat. We were all in our civvies, ready to dash for it, so we said to Bomber, 'Just block.' Wilf had this fast bowler on, and even he was told to bowl it wide of the stumps. 'We don't want to bat for one over,' he said. So this bloke bowls one wide of the off stump, and Bomber has a big swish and is caught. We all had to throw our whites on top of our other clothes."

"I only had the one shot, you see," Bomber says, and here at Cheltenham he plays it to the last ball of Johnny Wardle's over. "It pitched about leg, and I went to hit him over the top of square leg."

Bobby Etheridge has hit one six this over. Now Bomber aims another. The two boys from New Street, Gloucester. "His father worked with my Uncle Dave at Tom Morris's, the sand and gravel merchants." Ten years ago who would have thought that they would be out here together, trying to beat the mighty Yorkshire? *'Wells, promoted in the hope that he would provide one of his celebrated sixes, fell leg-before without scoring.'*

Gloucestershire's sudden attack has yielded nine runs in the over, but it has also brought two wickets. In the words of the Gloucestershire handbook, *'defeat seemed imminent.'*

Wells, lbw Wardle, 0   **Gloucestershire, 56 for eight**

David Smith joins Bobby Etheridge in the middle, two Bristol City footballers in the last weeks of their cricketing summer, and there is only Sam Cook to come. As the Echo reports, *'Romantic dreams of Cook coming out to hit the winning run in his benefit match came easily to mind now.'*

"He was as quiet as a church mouse," Bomber remembers.

"In those days," Tony Brown explains, "either you sat down outside or you stayed in the dressing room, where the windows were quite high. So, if you stayed inside, you had to stand on a seat to look out. And there he was. Very, very nervous. Smoking like the clappers."

Ten years ago Sam walked out to join Tom Goddard, the championship at stake. "Tom's eye was fiery," Bill Edrich wrote, "his lips compressed, his grip on his bat remorseless," but he drove the ball straight into Bill's hands and all Gloucestershire groaned. Forty years later Sam sat at home and began his autobiography, and he told how that long, hot summer of bowling had given him pains around his heart and that he only played Middlesex in that match on condition that he was lightly bowled. But *'faithful'* as ever, he sent down forty overs in two days, and there is just that one sentence to tell of their disappointment: "Tom went home and cried. I went home and got drunk."

The hand-written pages of Sam's memoir sit now among the photographs and newspaper cuttings that his daughter cherishes. So what are his memories of this benefit match in August 1957? On page 25 he ends his account of the summer of 1956, when the county finished third and briefly rekindled hopes of that still elusive championship. Then he moves on: *'The 1957 season was disappointing, dropping to twelfth position.'* And the writing stops. He has spent a lifetime in cricket, player and umpire, and nothing that he takes up in his retirement - gardening, photography, this writing - ever inspires him to the same dedication.

So we must imagine for ourselves how he feels as he stands on the chair and looks through the high window. A large crowd for his benefit, and the chance to beat Yorkshire in the hands of David Smith and Bobby Etheridge.

> *'There's a breathless hush in the close tonight,*
> *Ten to make and the match to win.'*

The words float across J.M. Kilburn's mind as he sits in the press tent beside the scoreboard, and he pens his report for the Yorkshire Post. *'The sunshine of the evening was pale, and the ball was keeping low rather than lifting dangerously. But if the details were different, the essential atmosphere of Sir Henry Newbolt was inescapable. Here on the school pitch Etheridge and Smith lived through overs of bumping pitch and blinding light with ten to make and the match to win.'*

John Bapty, with his shirtsleeves rolled up and his cigarette in his mouth, is scribbling, too: *'Thirteen to win, two wickets to fall. The close-in fielders hovered with outstretched hands.'* Two leg byes take the match total of extras conceded by Yorkshire to 37, compared with Gloucestershire's two, then *'Smith sliced a boundary through the slips'* and *'that brought the house down.'* At the other end *'Etheridge cut a genuine two off Illingworth,'* but the very next ball *'he was completely beaten'*. In the dressing room Sam Cook's heart leaps into his mouth.

'A breathless hush.' The ball beats Bobby Etheridge. It beats the stumps. Then, of all things, it beats *'poor Binks, who had been standing up to Illingworth.'*

"Poor old Binksy," Bomber says. "He didn't want to stand up, you know."

"He had to stand up," Ray Illingworth insists. "It was just one of those wickets it was impossible to keep on."

Bobby Etheridge is a wing-half at Bristol City, and he darts down the pitch for the first run, turns and sees *'the ball hit the fence'*. At this point *'he jumped with joy and scampered off the field.'* "That's it, gentlemen," the umpire Dai Davies says, and he and John Langridge pull up the stumps and follow the players off the field. The crowd cheers, there are a few indistinct shouts, and within moments *'children were swarming all over the pitch.'*

"If you ever beat Yorkshire," Bomber says, "it was the season's greatest feat."

Etheridge, not out, 12
Smith, not out, 4   **Gloucestershire, 68 for eight**

GLOUCESTERSHIRE

*G.M. Emmett	c Wilson b Illingworth	6
D.M. Young	c Stott b Wardle	9
R.B. Nicholls	c Binks b Wardle	7
T.W. Graveney	c Wilson b Wardle	5
C.A. Milton	c Trueman b Wardle	8
A.S. Brown	c Close b Wardle	0
J.B. Mortimore	c & b Illingworth	2
+R.J. Etheridge	not out	12
B.D. Wells	lbw b Wardle	0
D.R. Smith	not out	4
C. Cook		
Extras	*b 9, lb 6*	15
	(for 8 wickets)	**68**

1-18, 2-26, 3-30, 4-35, 5-39, 6-46, 7-56, 8-56

Trueman	2	0	12	0
Wardle	16	8	25	6
Illingworth	14.3	6	16	2

Wardle and Illingworth have made Gloucestershire struggle all the way, the one a seasoned professional, the other a young man still learning his game. Johnny has played his last Test for England, and in a year's time he will be sacked by Yorkshire in the interests of team spirit and greater discipline. Ray Illingworth, by contrast, is a year away from his first Test, and he remembers the end of the day here at Cheltenham when Johnny took him back out to the pitch

"When we bowled in the first innings," Ray recalls, "the wicket was wet but not doing much and we both had reasonable figures. But in the second I had about two for twenty, and Johnny had six. And he took me out and showed me the marks of the first innings. Where his marks all pitched within a yard of length, mine were more like two yards. And he said, 'That's why I cashed in more second time. Because I knocked it about more in the right place when it was wet in the first innings.' He was just proving the point of what you had to do when things weren't in your favour.

"Johnny may have been difficult on the field if things didn't go right for him, but he was also very helpful to young players."

Ray will play 61 Tests and become one of England's most successful captains.

Back in the Gloucestershire dressing room Sam Cook unbuckles his pads with relief. "Just before the end of the match," Tony Brown remembers, "the dressing room attendant would bring in a tray of drinks." At the end of a day like this, it does not take Sam long to down his first pint.

Are the celebrations wild in the Gloucestershire dressing room? "Oh no," Bomber says, and he recalls the day - maybe it is this game - when somebody at the end says, 'It's good to win.' "Old Emmett got up. 'It's good to lose, too,' he said. 'It keeps your feet on the ground. You should never gloat over winning.' He went on for about ten minutes about playing in the right spirit.

"People in Gloucestershire now just don't realise how much he did for the county when he was captain. He was magnificent."

"At the time," Tony Brown says, "we didn't realise what a good influence he was. I wish the youngsters now could be pushed and stretched like we were."

"George was a match winner," Arthur Milton says. "He and Jack Crapp were our mentors, and they both died quite young." Slowly the faces grow fewer at the old players' reunions. "I do miss him, you know. I'd just like to see him once or twice a year to revive old memories."

GOODBYE TO ALL THAT

The end of the game

The match is lost and won. Children swarm across the field as their fathers walk out to inspect the wicket. Picnic baskets are packed up, and the first spectators dash for the bus stops.

Back in the dressing room, Sam Cook downs his first pint. The takings for the two days are £1,464. Add on the collections, the Sunday matches and one or two dinners, and at the end of the summer he will have £3,067, just enough to have a bungalow built in Tetbury.

Benefits are larger in Yorkshire. Johnny Wardle will finish the summer with over £8,000. But the Yorkshire committee has a more paternalistic attitude towards their players. "They liked to keep the money safe," Ken Taylor says, "so they didn't let you have it straightaway." One poor player sees his takings invested in Australian shares and is left with almost nothing.

Sam's bungalow today

Sam's bungalow is one of a set of three on a lane running out of town. It is a comfortable bungalow with its own garage, though perhaps Sam has not earned quite enough to have it done to the highest standard. "He got some jerry builders," Bomber reckons. "Of all people, as a plumber, he should have known better. The roof capsized one night. He got up and hit his head on it, and the next morning he came down to Bristol with a great big bruise. The county had to loan him some money to have it put right."

"I don't know anything about that," his daughter Carol says. "That doesn't ring any bells." Perhaps it is just one of Bomber's stories, a little truth egged up into an entertaining yarn. Or is it? The present occupant stands at the door of the bungalow with a knowing smile. "Let's put it this way. There are a lot of alterations that have been done up there. I wouldn't like to say any more than that."

Sam plays on for another seven years, then in 1965 he joins the umpires' panel and in only his second game he is officiating at Lord's with John Langridge. Middlesex versus Nottinghamshire and, with just four minutes left, Bomber is at the wicket, last man in and six to win. "Cometh the hour, cometh the man," Sam whispers to him. "Here's a chance for you to make a name for yourself." Bomber recalls the end: "I was caught by Peter Parfitt at gully. A magnificent catch. Quite wasted on me. 'Bad luck me old mate,' Sam said. 'That's one more you can put down to experience.'"

Sam does just one year on the panel before his wife's illness forces him to return to plumbing. But in 1971 he becomes an umpire again, and he does another sixteen years to the age of 65. "He was well-respected," Bomber says. "Well-liked, too. You'll never hear anybody say anything bad about Sam." And does he achieve his ambition to become "the sharpest bloody finger in the country"? Tom Graveney chuckles: "He used to swear when people swept him off the stumps. But he got his own back as an umpire. If they missed and it was somewhere near, it was out."

"I always liked to bowl at his end," Essex's Robin Hobbs told me. "He gave Boycott out one day when he'd got 233. It was no way out. 'That's out,' Sam said, and Boycott was running this leg bye. 'No, no, no, Sam,' he said. 'That can't be lbw.' 'That's out,' Sam said, and he turned to me. 'I think we've seen enough of *him*.'"

"The umpires looked after the game," Bomber says.

"The travelling is the hardest part of the job," Sam tells John Arlott on that television interview. "You can cover about ten thousand miles a season. When you're a player, you always have company, but an umpire's life can be very lonely."

"He took to coming home at night," his son-in-law Richard says. "From as far away as Hove and Northampton."

In his last summer as an umpire they allocate him to the Cheltenham Festival and once more he drives over the hill at Painswick and down into the familiar, tree-lined streets around the college. Almost forty years have passed since Middlesex came here and beat them to the championship, and fate has it that this last game here is against Middlesex, with 'the Gloucesters' once more at the top of the table. What was it Dai Davies said at Bournemouth in 1948? "That's out, and we've won the championship." Sam is too quiet a man for such partisan exuberance, but in any case there is no opportunity. In a rain-ruined match, Gloucestershire chase 357 and are all out for 252. Runners-up for the sixth time since 1930. Six times third as well. And still no title.

"The last time he ever umpired," Richard says, "was when the Australians came to Arundel in 1989. I had to persuade him to do it. I drove him over there, and I don't think he went back out after tea."

Lavinia, the Duchess of Norfolk's Eleven against the Australians. A gloriously hot day at Arundel Castle. A swarm of bees stops play, one of Allan Border's sixes breaks a lady's nose, and the loudspeaker interrupts play with messages about dogs in distress in parked cars. Sam's fellow umpire is a 79-year-old John Langridge, whose Wisden obituary could have been written with this day in mind: *'As he aged, his complexion grew more apple-red and he seemed, alongside Sam Cook, to represent everything that was best about county cricket.'*

£3,000 in 1957 for the *'faithful'* Sam Cook, enough for him to move out of his council house. £300,000 in 1999 for Mike Atherton. "I don't think county cricket serves any purpose whatsoever," he tells Radio Five soon afterwards. "Very few people turn up to watch, it doesn't prepare people for a higher level of cricket, and it doesn't attract TV deals or sponsorship. It's living on borrowed time."

"I worry about county cricket," Tom Graveney says. "I can see it disappearing."

"I wouldn't pay to watch Atherton," Bomber says. "All these dab shots. He rarely executes a beautiful cover drive. There's no personality in his batting. But Hammond …"

"I know, I know, Bomber. You've told me about Hammond."

"Or Denis Compton. I bowled this swinger to him. It started just outside leg, and he went down on one knee to play the old sweep. Then, just as he was about to play, he shouted 'the swinger' and hit it through extra cover for four. I said, 'Christ, Denis, if you'd missed that, it would have hit all three down.' He said, 'You're a slow bowler. That'll teach you to bowl slow.' What a shot!"

The summer of 1957. Denis Compton retires, a quartet of great leg-break bowlers leave without replacement, and Gloucestershire's finances plummet deeper into the red. When George Emmett retires at the end of 1958, Tom Graveney succeeds him, but behind the scenes a benefactor is bailing out the county and at the end of 1960 the players discover with shock that his son has been appointed captain.

"I did the post that Christmas," John Light recalls. "My first stop was the Lodge at Highgrove, my second the house itself. I'd cycled out from Tetbury in the freezing cold, and they used to take me into the huge kitchen with the Aga and warm me up with coffee and mince pies. Then I went on back to Tetbury, and Cooky's bungalow was on my round. All the players had left at the end of the season, thinking that Arthur Milton was going to be the captain. You should have heard what he had to say about it all."

So Tom Pugh takes over in 1961, and Tom Graveney leaves for Worcester. It is 1969 before this happy, home-grown Gloucestershire side sorts out its captaincy, when Tony Brown takes over. But by then they are not so home-grown and, when they win the Gillette Cup in 1973, the first four in the batting are Sadiq Mohammad, Roger Knight, Zaheer Abbas and Mike Procter. Two Pakistanis, a South African and a transfer from Surrey.

Those same ten years, 1959 to 1968, when Gloucestershire are lurching from one captain to another, yield Yorkshire seven championship titles, and the young players emerging here at Cheltenham - Ray Illingworth, Jimmy Binks, Doug Padgett, Bryan Stott - become some of the cornerstones of that success. 1959 to 1968, these are the last years before the Sunday League brings a reduction in the championship programme, the last years before the English county game looks overseas for its star players, and the pace of change quickens when in 1970 Yorkshire sack their captain Brian Close, citing his lack of belief in the one-day game.

"Look at it now," he says. "Captains take a bowler off or put him on, they have to go and have a five-minute chat, placing the field and all that. We used to do that between balls. And if a fellow didn't look as if he was taking wickets, 'Right, put your sweater on.' Another bowler was straight on. We had variety in the attack. We gave the batsmen different problems all the time. But they don't know how to do it now because of the influence of the one-day game. 'Oh well, we've so many overs to bowl so we'll take our time.' I told them thirty years ago. It's been the ruination of cricket."

"Limited over cricket," Bomber says. "Neville Cardus said to me, it's like trying to play Beethoven on a banjo."

In 1999 Gloucestershire play 17 championship matches and 27 one-day games and, in Bomber's words, "cricket now is full of all these itsy-bitsy players, trundlers who bat a bit." Of this 1957 side, George Emmett would be considered too old, his gammy knees a handicap in the field. Bomber would never get beyond club cricket in Gloucester, overweight and not coached through the county's youth schemes. Arthur Milton would have opted for football, along with Bobby Etheridge, Ron Nicholls and David Smith, and John Mortimore would be playing too much over-limit cricket to develop his flight. Tom Graveney does not think he could play without the rhythm of batting four times a week. And Sam Cook? What about Sam? "You could go back two hundred years, and you would find chaps like Sam Cook playing cricket." Today? Who knows? They would certainly be advising him on his diet.

"I suppose cricket has changed more than any other sport in history," Bomber says. "Now we've got this Lord MacLaurin, and he's falling into the same trap. Trying to rush through all these changes. And it all seems to be about marketing. But it's not a supermarket."

Brian Close agrees. "The trouble is, the game doesn't come first these days, does it? The money comes first."

August 1957. Harold Macmillan says we have never had it so good, Elvis Presley is 'All Shook Up' at the top of the Hit Parade, and the first £1,000 premium bond prizes are drawn. Here at Cheltenham the game is over, and the players plan their day off.

"Golf tomorrow at Cotswold Hills?" Tom Graveney asks Arthur Milton.

Bobby Etheridge packs his bag. His brief hour of glory over, he will return to training with Bristol City. On Wednesday, in another benefit match for Sam, George Emmett will keep wicket and Bobby will be on the opposition, playing for Bristol City, who hold out for a draw, thanks to a *'defiant'* 30 not out by John Atyeo. Then on Saturday the City will lose 2-1 at home to Liverpool, and *'both inside-forwards, Etheridge and Atyeo, played like men who could do with a little more ball practice.'*

Peter Rochford has played his last game for the county, and the opening is there for either Bobby Etheridge or Barrie Meyer. Tony Brown remembers the conversation. "'What do you want to do, Bobby?' George Emmett asked him. 'Do you want to go and play football? If you do, Barrie will come in and be the keeper.'" Bobby is never again Gloucestershire's first-choice behind the stumps.

Barrie Meyer plays for the Rovers, but he puts cricket first and he is the county's keeper till 1971, eight years after Bobby ends with the City. "I think later on," Bomber says, "Eth would have given anything to have won his county cap."

The game is over.

At Cheltenham in 1999 the scene is still much the same, a place *'where people renew friendships and discover why they fell in love with cricket.'* But the young farm workers, who played with Charles Light, even with his son John, are not there now, and the audience is older, more affluent. Gone are the boys sitting around the boundary rope.

The Cheltenham Festival survives, but Chesterfield and Harrogate no longer stage county cricket, nor do Bournemouth and Weston-super-Mare. Everywhere, it seems, the accountants and marketing men are proposing change: two divisions, 20-over evening matches, floodlights, counties amalgamating, regional cricket, central contracts for England players, the hosting of overseas Test series.

I listen with pleasure to the old cricketers talking. I had no idea what a nerve I would touch with my book on the 1950s. Giving voice once more to the last generation who played their sport before the money took over. We don't want to hear them now, do we? We don't want them telling us that we have got our values wrong.

What was it the man said to Charles Light in the woods? "I could have listened to you all day, Charlie. These young people are all piss and wind."

"I'm very sad about it all," Arthur Milton says. "Because the game I loved has gone. Gone. The whole spirit of life is not the same, is it?"

So was it all better in 1957?

"I don't know," Bomber says. "Maybe, as you get older and you watch the young people playing, you start to have the wrong thoughts."

THE SOONER THE BETTER

In the marquee

The summer of 1999. It is fifty years now since a nine-year-old John Light arrived for the first time at this ground, saw Laker bowl Jack Crapp - or was he stumped? - and began a lifelong love affair with this Festival. Now he is Chairman of the Gloucestershire Exiles, and the fourth and final day of the Worcestershire match is the occasion of their annual reunion.

As Michael Henderson wrote in the Telegraph, *'it is a ground peopled by exiles who have come home.'*

Mark Alleyne in the centre, with Bomber behind his left shoulder.

Lunch approaches. Inside the marquee the tables are set for a hundred guests. Outside, the Gloucestershire innings is withering away. Just one second innings wicket remains, and they are still 65 runs from making Worcestershire bat again. "Why on earth did Mark Alleyne put them in?" everybody is asking as they leave the morning sunshine for the Exiles lunch.

At their 1996 and '97 lunches Bomber entertained them with his tales - of the over he bowled while the clock struck twelve, the catch he took with a tea cup in his hand, the day Wilf Wooller threatened to eat his hat. But in '98 he lay in the Gloucestershire Royal Hospital, fighting his way back from a debilitating stroke, and the decision was taken to do without a speaker.

Here in 1999 we settle to lunch, and Bomber and Mary sit at the next table, his sticks lying on the grass at his feet. Now I have been asked to talk to the Exiles after lunch, and I am sitting beside John Light. Anxiously I look around the marquee till the Exiles Treasurer draws me into conversation.

"So which of the cricketers in *Runs in the Memory* did you most enjoy interviewing?"

How can I compare them with each other? The ever-generous Bomber, with his endless fund of hilarious stories, or the religious Dickie Dodds, challenging me to look into my heart? Tom Cartwright, the dedicated craftsman, or Ken Biddulph, with his ever-observant eye? Or Bryan Stott, almost in tears as he relives Yorkshire's 1959 triumph?

"I did enjoy interviewing Arthur Milton," I say finally.

"Ah," the Treasurer smiles. "I thought you'd say that."

The meal over-runs the forty-minute interval and, by the time we are finished, there are cheers outside as Ball and Lewis make carefree runs for the tenth wicket. "Let's go outside and enjoy it while it lasts," John suggests. "Then we can all come back and listen to Stephen."

"I've written up a brief story of the 1957 game here against Yorkshire," I say, not sure how long they want me to speak. "Perhaps I could start by telling you how I came to write my two books. Then, if the game is all over, I'll read you the story."

Ball and Lewis. *'This pair could have taught Puff the Magic Dragon a few things about frolicking,'* Rob Steen writes in the Sunday Telegraph, and before long Playfair Annuals are being pulled out of pockets. Gloucestershire, partnership records, tenth wicket, 131 by Gouldsworthy and Bessant versus Somerset in 1923. They have reached 130 when - to a universal groan - Lewis is bowled, and we all retire into the tent. Worcestershire need 65 to win, a mere formality. The glasses of wine are refilled, and John introduces me. On the next table Bomber's eyes twinkle through his thick glasses.

"I didn't want to interview the big names like Freddie Trueman and Trevor Bailey," I say, starting to get into my stride. "I wanted to catch the memories of the county stalwarts, the cricketers whose voices we never hear. People like Martin Horton at Worcester, Ken Taylor of Yorkshire, Arthur Milton in Bristol.

"Arthur Milton," I repeat with a wistful sigh. "The last man to play cricket and football for England. When he retired, he became a postman. I wonder what life he would lead today as a double international, what adverts he'd appear on, what fees his agent would charge for magazine interviews and chat show appearances. I rang him up, and I arranged to go and see him. 'What time would you like to come?' he asked. "Well, I'll come early if you like. Say, nine o'clock.' 'No, don't come that early,' he said. 'I've got three paper rounds to get done.' Three paper rounds! The last man to play cricket and football for England."

I draw breath for a moment.

"I wonder," I continue. "Ben Hollioake. Do you think he'll ever do a paper round?"

From the next table comes a loud whisper, with a strong Gloucester burr. "The sooner the better."

"I've written a short piece about the Yorkshire game here in 1957," I say. "I thought I'd read you some of it." I pick up my papers and begin the story. *'The Gloucestershire team emerges, led as custom demands by Sam Cook. "Didn't he*

117

get a cheer?" Bomber laughs. "I think the old lad was rather embarrassed."' Outside the marquee, there is a shout and a roar, and somebody sitting by the flap announces, "Weston's out."

I press on. *'Emmett deserved so many more hundreds than he got. Other people played for them, but he didn't. He played exactly the same from start to finish, and they're the kind of people you remember, aren't they?'* The roar from outside the marquee returns. "Two down."

"Carry on," John Light says, looking round at the Exiles, who are all absorbed in this lost world of 1957. So I progress to the morning of the second day. *'Wells disturbed the members of the local constitutional club with a deliciously rustic six .... "The ball was taking off, going over Binksy's head." ... "I can see Eth now. He was all skin and bone, but he wanted to get out there, show them who was boss."'* Now there is a third roar, greater than the other two, and the news is relayed in to us. "Hick's out. It's thirteen for three."

I hurry forward to the finish of my 1957 match. *'Romantic dreams of Cook coming out to hit the winning run came easily to mind now. ... The ball went for four byes. Etheridge leapt high in delight, and the players left the field.'*

I sit down, and another roar from outside the marquee interrupts the applause. "Solanki's out."

The Exiles hurry back to the sunshine of 1999, and I am left to sign a few books and sit down beside Bomber.

"Was it all right?" I ask.

"It was very good," he says. "They're such lovely people, aren't they? And it was a lovely meal, too, wasn't it, Mary?"

By the time I emerge from the marquee, blinking with the brightness of the sun, the game is almost over. For a brief moment we dream that we might be here on one of those days which will remain in people's memories all their lives. Days like that one when Cliff Monks ran forty yards to pluck the ball off the heads of the crowd, or when the mysterious Sonny Ramadhin mesmerised the pride of the county's batting, or when Bobby Etheridge swung Johnny Wardle away for six. *'The day Ball and Lewis put on 130 for the last wicket, then they came out and bowled Worcester out for 62.'*

Alas, it is not to be. The 66 runs are scored, and the players leave the field.

Cricket in 1999. It still draws us back.

"If you love the game," Bomber says, "you'll never lose that enthusiasm. It will dampen, but you'll never lose it."

ONE MORE RUN

Looking back one last time

I have written two books about county cricket: *Runs in the Memory* and *Caught in the Memory*. "What's the next one going to be called?" someone asked me. "*Stumped for a Memory? Run Out of Memories?*" "No," I said, "I think I've done enough cricket memories. Time to move on to something new." But Bomber persuaded me to write a book with him, and here we are, giving it one more run.

We started in Spring 1998 with long sessions on his childhood - "I used to sit there listening to them, and I never realised how your brain stores away all the information." - and his days of club cricket - "You had to take your turn on the roller or painting the boundary, and it didn't do you any harm. You appreciated the game more by helping to create it." Then in the June, just as I was clearing the decks for a real burst on it, Mary rang me. "Bryan's had a stroke. It's quite a bad one. I'll understand it if you don't want to carry on with the book."

Eleven weeks in Gloucestershire Royal Hospital. Eleven weeks of getting some movement back in his legs, some coherence back in his voice. But he never lost his cheerful, fighting spirit. "When we went back for physio," Mary says, "we met a couple of the nurses. 'I wish you'd come back again, Bomber,' they said. 'It's so miserable without you.'"

"How is Bomber?" Tom Graveney asks me when I see him. "He's a lot better," I say. "But he's not very mobile." Tom laughs: "He never was, was he?"

"What did you do for a living?" one of the nurses asks Bomber one day. "I was a cricketer," he replies. "I played for Gloucestershire." "Ah," she says. "You must have known my uncle Sam."

Sam Cook. His body lies in the churchyard in Tetbury, down in the far corner by the wall. When the old cricketers attended his funeral, Arthur Milton smiled sadly. "Still down at third man, I see, Sam."

Forty years earlier, Sam was downing a pint at Cheltenham, happy that the sun had shone for his benefit, happy that they had beaten Yorkshire and happy that he had not had to bat. *'Children ran all over the pitch, and the ground was swarming with people.'*

It is all over. The ball has run for four byes, Bobby Etheridge has *'jumped with joy and scampered from the field'*, and Gloucestershire are celebrating "the season's greatest feat", victory over Yorkshire.

It is almost half a century since Yorkshire last came to Cheltenham and it will be nearly a quarter more before they come again. Not Emmett facing Trueman now but Boycott against Procter, as one old Gloucestershire member recalls. "It was a very still day, and I can still hear the crack of his bat as he hooked him." Then Boycott reaches the non-striker's end, and Procter completes a hat-trick of lbws. "I had a Yorkshireman standing next to me in the new club tents. And he said, 'None of them would have been out if Dickie Bird had been umpiring.'"

Cheltenham memories. The young men play their cricket, hardly aware of the ghosts that the older spectators see all around them.

But wait a moment! There were shouts as the players left the field in 1957. Did you notice them? They were coming from the scorers and the press tent. Beside the plain-faced, portable scoreboard with its guy ropes. Maybe you were shouting. It was 69 to win, and Gloucestershire have only scored 68. Their first innings total is wrong on the scoreboard, and the game is not over at all.

Fred Aubrey hurries across to the gymnasium. He is a retired bank manager, and his book does not balance. "You shouldn't have come off," he tells the umpires. "It was 69 to win. They need one more run."

"The crowd were leaving in their hundreds," Bomber says.

"It was total confusion," Tony Brown recalls. "Dear old Fred Aubrey arrived, and he started talking to the umpires."

"Dai Davies was the one who told us we had to go back out," Bomber remembers. "He was a jolly man, always joking, but he was very apologetic when he came in. The pair of them were quite sheepish."

The Stop Press in the Echo tells the story in staccato:
'With score at 64-8 the ball went for four byes … Etheridge leapt high in delight and the players left the field … Swarms of children ran over the pitch … Then it was realised another run was needed … The field was cleared and the players reappeared … Umpire Langridge without the ball.'

John Bapty elaborates: *'The stumps were replaced, police shooed the last small boys back behind the boundary, and the players resumed their positions. There followed a further delay because the umpires had forgotten the ball.'*

Ray Illingworth has three deliveries remaining in his over and, once John Langridge has returned with the ball, the game resumes. Three balls, three dots in Fred Aubrey's scorebook, and once more Johnny Wardle will bowl to David Smith.

Back in the dressing room, there is another detail, not visible from the press tent but captured in the county handbook: *'Sam Cook frantically buckled on his pads again.'*

"People love stories, don't they?" Bomber says.

When George Lambert tucked into the free drinks here that lunch-time, he came in to bowl the first ball after lunch and he ran straight into the wickets. And when Sam enjoyed himself at Badminton that Sunday, he spent the afternoon falling over at third man. Now here at Cheltenham, he is padding up and, according to Ray Illingworth, "he'd downed his pint in three seconds flat."

What better an ending could the story have than for Sam to step out here in his benefit match, nine wickets down and one run to win, the great Johnny Wardle with the ball in his hand and the beer spinning round his head.
'My hands are shaking, and my knees are weak,
I can't seem to stand on my own two feet,
… I'm all shook up.'

Arthur Milton laughs: "Probably he'd be better off with the pint."

David Smith plays the first ball of the over back down the pitch, and the tension mounts. This is the young David's fifth innings against Yorkshire, and his snick for four before they came off has taken his total of runs against them to eight. To the second ball of the over, according to the Echo's Stop Press, *'Smith had a wild swing at Wardle and missed.'* Sam is on the chair now, looking through the high window *'The ball shaved the off stump.'* Oh no, he really is going to have to bat. And there won't be an easy long hop to get him off the mark this time.

But the bail does not fall, *'the ball eluded the wicket-keeper'* and *'the rest was anti-climax'*. Another bye, the thirtieth Jimmy Binks has conceded, and this time there is no victory leap from Bobby Etheridge. The umpires pull up the stumps, and the players leave the field a second time. Away on the far side Fred Aubrey starts to total up his book.

GLOUCESTERSHIRE

*G.M. Emmett	c Wilson b Illingworth	6
D.M. Young	c Stott b Wardle	9
R.B. Nicholls	c Binks b Wardle	7
T.W. Graveney	c Wilson b Wardle	5
C.A. Milton	c Trueman b Wardle	8
A.S. Brown	c Close b Wardle	0
J.B. Mortimore	c & b Illingworth	2
+R.J. Etheridge	not out	12
B.D. Wells	lbw b Wardle	0
D.R. Smith	not out	4
C. Cook		
Extras	*b 10, lb 6*	16
	(for 8 wickets)	**69**

1-18, 2-26, 3-30, 4-35, 5-39, 6-46, 7-56, 8-56

Trueman	2	0	12	0
Wardle	16.2	8	25	6
Illingworth	15	6	16	2

"Where we probably lost," Ray Illingworth says, "was in not bringing me on straightaway. We didn't want to give any runs away with George Emmett sweeping but, when I came on, I got him out in my first over. If we'd gambled on that earlier, we'd have won the match. But you're always wise after the event."

We are all wise after the event.

Bomber sits in his wheelchair, waiting for the crowds to thin out before he takes up his sticks. "My dad and his four brothers sat there," he remembers. "All of them drank. And all the time they'd be talking about cricket. Picking their best England team, that sort of thing. And the more they had to drink, the more

Gloucestershire players there'd be in the side. And I just listened. I never realised it, the actual effect it was having on me at the time."

Tony Brown has retired from his post at Lord's, pensioned off when Lord MacLaurin took over. "George Emmett was a martinet, a great disciplinarian," he says. "When you're being chased from pillar to post, all the good parts of the game are being ingrained in you. We didn't realise what a good influence he was having on us. He was marvellous."

Tom Graveney is recovering from a new hip and the insertion of a pacemaker. "I love talking cricket," he says. "It's a great game. A great game."

Cheltenham in 1957. Young boys swarming across the field. Farm labourers from the village cricket teams. Country vicars. Holiday-makers from all over. And old men with memories of Jessop and Hammond.

"Lord MacLaurin's got no idea," Bomber says. "There have always been doddery old men at cricket. They can spend their leisure hours, watching it, passing their lives away. You get keen young men and women, but in time they will become old and they'll see a different game."

Sam Cook's benefit match in 1957. How Bomber loves to tell the story! But his eyes never leave the game in front of him in 1999. "I've told Matt Windows, he should be in the England team, but he's got to stop stepping to leg and cutting."

At the King's School or on Gloucester Spa, here at Cheltenham or around the Cotswold villages, you will still find him in his wheelchair, watching the cricket. Still looking for that natural talent that has grown up away from all the coaching schemes and the sponsored cars.

"What are you looking for, Bomber? How do you know when you see real talent?"

He stares across the emptying field, where the groundsman is sweeping the square. He stares back through the years, where Hammond and Walcott, Emmett and Solanki are all playing before him. A lifetime of listening and talking, of watching and playing.

"You get a tingling feeling in the nape of your neck."

'Somewhere there's music - how faint the tune.
Somewhere there's heaven - how high the moon.'

"Come on, Bryan," Mary says. "Let's get going."

"Would you like an apple, Stephen, for the journey home?"

"No, it's all right, thank you, Bomber."

"Go on, take it."

I walk back to my car, relishing every bite.

What was it he said?

"It's the funniest, loveliest game under the sun if you just let people get on with it."

ACKNOWLEDGEMENTS

I would like to express my thanks to all those who shared their memories with me. Without their help this book could not have been written.

In particular, I spoke to Colin Auger, Tony Brown, Brian Close, Carol Cooper, Nico Craven, Geoff Edrich, Sally Feal, Gill Ford, Roger Ford, Tom Graveney, Derek Hawkins, Len Hemming, Ray Illingworth, Charles Light, John Light, Joyce McMurray, Arthur Milton, Rt Rev & Rt Hon Lord (David) Sheppard, Bryan Stott, Ken Taylor, Norman Tyson and, of course, Bomber and Mary Wells.

I would like to thank David T. Smith for his meticulous and perceptive proof-reading, Bert Avery at the County Ground in Bristol for lending me the scorebook and scorecard, and Grenville Simons, who is currently writing a history of cricket at Cheltenham.

I would particularly like to thank Carol Cooper for allowing me to read and quote from her father Sam Cook's unfinished memoir *Bowling Down The Road*.

I have made regular use of the following reference books:
Wisden Cricketers' Almanack
News Chronicle and Daily Dispatch Cricket Annual 1957
Bailey, Thorn & Wynne-Thomas, *Who's Who of Cricketers*
      (Newnes Books, 1984)
Robert Brooke, *A History of the County Cricket Championship*
      (Guinness, 1991)
Jim Ledbetter & Peter Wynne-Thomas, *First-Class Cricket, 1931-39*
      (Limlow Books, 9 volumes, 1991-9)

I have also read and occasionally quoted from the following books:
John Arlott, *Vintage Summer: 1947* (Eyre & Spottiswoode, 1957)
Derek Birley, *The Willow Wand* (Queen Anne Press, 1979)
Brian Close, *I Don't Bruise Easily* (Macdonald & Jane's, 1978)
Nico Craven, *A Watching Brief* (privately published, 1995)
Dickie Dodds, *Hit Hard And Enjoy It* (The Cricketer, 1976)
W.J. Edrich, *Cricket Heritage* (Stanley Paul, 1948)
Alan Gibson, *Growing Up With Cricket* (George Allen & Unwin, 1985)
Tom Graveney, *Cricket Through The Covers* (Frederick Muller, 1958)
David Green, *The History of Gloucestershire* (Christopher Helm, 1990)
Alan Hill, *Johnny Wardle, Cricket Conjuror* (David & Charles, 1988)
Frank Keating, *Half-Time Whistle* (Robson Books, 1992)
Laurie Lee, *Cider with Rosie* (Hogarth Press, 1959)
Patrick Murphy, *The Centurions* (J.M. Dent & Sons, 1983)
Grahame Parker, *Gloucestershire Road* (Pelham Books, 1983)
Mike Stevenson, *Illingworth* (Ward Lock, 1978)
Bomber Wells, *Well, Well, Wells* (Cabdene, 1981)

also from the following newspapers:
The Times, Daily Telegraph, News Chronicle, Bristol Evening Post, Gloucester Citizen, Gloucestershire Echo, Stroud News and Journal, Western Daily Press, Yorkshire Post and Yorkshire Evening Post.

and from the following cricket magazines:
The Cricketer, Playfair Cricket Monthly and Wisden Cricket Monthly.

STATISTICAL NOTE

On page 101, I state that the four-day match in 1999 would have ended on the third evening if the players had bowled their overs at the same rate as in 1957. For those who like to check these things, I have calculated as follows:

The 1957 match saw 224.2 overs bowled in 650 minutes, a rate of 20.7 overs per hour. The 1999 match contained 403.2 overs which, at a rate of 20.7 per hour, would take 19½ hours plus ½ hour for the three changes of innings. The playing conditions for 1999 allocated 6½ hours a day, with an additional ½ hour available on any of the first three evenings if the match is nearing completion, so this means that the match could be completed by taking the extra ½ hour on the third evening.

The rate of 20.7 overs per hour was not exceptional in Gloucestershire matches in 1957. In fact, in the game against Warwickshire at Bristol, the teams sustained a rate of 22.6 overs per hour. At that rate the 1999 match would have finished over an hour before the scheduled close on the third day.

Stephen Chalke
Bath, May 2000

CAUGHT IN THE MEMORY -
COUNTY CRICKET IN THE 1960s

by Stephen Chalke

with illustrations by Ken Taylor

A second innings as salty, charming and free flowing as the first.

Colin Chinery, Eastern Daily Press

I thought Mr Chalke could never repeat his success. He has. Triumphantly. 'Caught in the Memory' is a delight. Read the book. Read the book, I beg you. I commend it wholeheartedly - and not least for the splendid illustrations by Mr Ken Taylor. He won't remember, but once he trod on my toe in the tea interval at Bramall Lane. He could grind my whole body into the ground without trace if he compels Mr Chalke to produce another volume.

Peter Tinniswood, Wisden Cricketers' Almanack

Chalke clearly has a huge respect and liking for professional cricketers, and his finest achievement is the marvellous way in which he brings characters to life. He gives accounts of a dozen separate games and, if you weren't there at the time, by the end you feel as though you were. Sports books don't get any better.

Steve Simpson, Blackpool Gazette

Both books are in hardback and are available post free from Fairfield Books, 17 George's Road, Fairfield Park, Bath BA1 6EY.   Telephone 01225-335813

Runs in the Memory: £15.95   **Caught in the Memory: £16.95**

Chalke's success has done wonders for the independent self-publisher.

Frank Keating, The Oldie